beside
you

beside
you

*how Lukas' special needs
revealed mine*

Kimberly L. Sanders

Heavenly
Light Press
Alpharetta, GA

The author has tried to recreate events, locations, and conversations from her memories of them. In some instances, in order to maintain their anonymity, the author has changed the names of individuals and places. She may also have changed some identifying characteristics and details such as physical attributes, occupations, and places of residence.

Copyright © 2021 by Kimberly L. Sanders

ISBN: 978-1-6653-0054-4 - Paperback
eISBN: 978-1-6653-0055-1 - ePub
eISBN: 978-1-6653-0056-8 - mobi

Printed in the United States of America   062821

⊛This paper meets the requirements of ANSI/NISO Z39.48-1992 (Permanence of Paper)

Scripture quotations marked "NIV" are taken from the Holy Bible, New International Version®, NIV®. Copyright © 1973, 1978, 1984 by Biblica, Inc.™ Used by permission of Zondervan. All rights reserved worldwide.

To Lukas ~
You are a gift in beautiful wrappings,
my unexpected treasure

Table of Contents

The Story   ix

Part I. This Little Light   1
Chapter 1. Choose   3
Chapter 2. Great Expectations   7
Chapter 3. This Little Light of Mine   15

Part II. Hide Him   19
Chapter 4. Nouns First   21
Chapter 5. Manna for the Day   23
Chapter 6. Just Be Mom   29
Chapter 7. The Lurking Monster   33
Chapter 8. IEP and the Slipping Banner   35
Chapter 9. For Nothing Is Impossible with God   41
Chapter 10. At the Core   45
Chapter 11. The Bubble   49
Chapter 12. Pull up a Chair   53
Chapter 13. A Double Life   57
Chapter 14. Silent Speaking   67
Chapter 15. Special Needs Indeed   71

Part III. Blow Him Out   75
Chapter 16. Re-member   77
Chapter 17. Walls Won't Win   83
Chapter 18. Not Such Bright Horizons   89
Chapter 19. Mirrored Pain   93
Chapter 20. Hands Full or Handful?   97
Chapter 21. Training for Two   99

Chapter 22. Abandon   105
Chapter 23. Armor of God   109
Chapter 24. Losing Control   113
Chapter 25. Power of a Name   117
Chapter 26. Start with our Toes   121
Chapter 27. Kind to Our Core   125
Chapter 28. Weighty Matters   129
Chapter 29. Training for Two Continues   135
Chapter 30. Stable Sitting   139

Part IV. Let Him Shine   **143**
Chapter 31. It is Quite Simple, Really   145
Chapter 32. Living in Your Lane   147
Chapter 33. Reworking Routine into Ritual   151
Chapter 34. Beauty in the Wading   155
Chapter 35. Call of the One   159
Chapter 36. Dread into Dancing   163
Chapter 37. The Mantra   167
Chapter 38. Marriage: Shared, Divided,
            and Multiplied   171
Chapter 39. Only in Hindsight   175
Chapter 40. The Unnamed Ingredients   179
Chapter 41. Roll Call   183
Chapter 42. The Great Physician   187

Epilogue   *191*
Thank You   *193*
An Afterword   *195*
Endnotes   *197*
Glossary   *201*

The Story

Before I introduce you to my son Lukas, the real guide of this book, I thought I should tell you a little bit about myself.

I am someone who met my beau, my truest of loves, later in life. I wish I knew him in his youth, but we laugh and admit that we probably wouldn't have liked each other back then. We grew up in the same hometown of Crystal Lake, about sixty miles northwest of Chicago, and we attended the same middle and high schools. Yet we didn't meet until twenty years later. For a girl who is not great with technology, it feels strange to say that I met Eric online. I somehow envisioned meeting my future husband on an airplane, traveling to some offbeat, international country. But instead I first saw Eric as I sat before my computer dressed in pjs, with remnants of yesterday's make-up on, and my hair in a sloppy ponytail. Not the story I anticipated.

Before Eric walked into my life, I was immersed in various creative fields: dance, theater, and literature. I loved learning about other people through story and then embodying those lives through dance and theater. I later became a high school English teacher and learned about my students' lives through their writing and fictional characters' lives through the novels we studied. Only recently have I realized that storytelling is a thread that runs through all of my loves.

Perhaps it is this love of story that led me to share Lukas' story with you. The stories of those who have gone before me on this Down syndrome path have buoyed me when I needed hope or humor, and they helped me when I needed sobering truth or guidance. And after voraciously taking in all I could find, I realized it was my turn to join the conversation.

I always longed to be called Mom one day. Lukas gave me that gift. He started a new journey for me. This new storyline is one I most often feel unequipped to live out, but one I am so thankful for in the midst. This is not the story I thought I would have--being a stepmom, a mom of a son with Down syndrome, and a mom of an adopted daughter. But this is the story I love.

It shook me, stretched me, shaped me, and I think all for good.

Join me for the story...

Part I

This Little Light
sparks of love

"The giving of love is an education in itself."
— Eleanor Roosevelt

"We are shaped and fashioned by what we love."
— Johann Wolfgang von Goethe

Chapter 1

Choose

We had a coveted hallway at my high school called "Jock Hall." Its name tells it all really. It bustled with star athletes and popular students as they carved their way toward their lockers. The school must have caught on to how exclusive and hurtful this hallway could be because they have since replaced the lockers with trophy cases and the hall no longer bears its former name. However, back in the mid 80's when I was there, this was the hallway that had prospective seniors camping out the night before school started to reserve a locker. We literally pulled an all-nighter in the school's parking lot as if we were lining up for concert tickets. It wasn't that we wanted to see someone famous, we wanted to become someone "famous."

As a freshman, I avoided this hallway at all costs. To brush shoulders with these seniors left me with staccato breaths. They knew I was out of place and so just walking in their midst made me feel a heightened timidity. If I accidentally went this way, I would make myself small: my head hung low, my shoulders rolled in, and I found the books I was carrying fascinating!

Yet when I was a sophomore, I started to become intrigued with this hallway. I relished walking down it just to catch a glimpse of the couples that emerged. The girl often with her back against the locker and the boy leaning toward her just waiting for an opportunity to press in with a kiss. They never looked awkward to me; they appeared to be experts at flirting. The girl often giggled and played coy, while the boy steadfastly pursued her.

There is one couple I can still imagine walking down that hall—Randy and Diane. He wore his football jersey and feathered back hair, and she wore her cheerleading outfit and long lashes. They seldom engaged in public affection, but I yearned to have what she had. Randy? No. I loved his quick wit and upbeat personality, but it wasn't about being romantically drawn to him. There was some other reason this couple caught my eye. Even though I found them mismatched, somehow they are still the couple that comes to mind when I think about what I longed for in those high school days.

And this longing wasn't only as I watched couples, but it would also emerge as I traipsed between friend groups. Why did I want to be in Maureen's group so badly when Jenny's group was the one including me in their activities? It felt like the waters of high school just naturally pushed me alongside Jenny and friends, but the inevitability of this kept it from being as appealing. I was more drawn to being a part of Maureen's group, which seemed so unlikely. Why did I feel this way? It was...? What *is* that desire that consumes us in our teens? And what is that desire that continues to stir in me even now?

Many years later, I have come to realize that what I really longed for was to be chosen. I yearned to feel like one of those girls that had a boy selecting her out of the crowd. And when it all felt so unlikely, like it did with Randy and Diane, I found it more compelling. I didn't want to be with a guy or a group because it made sense, I wanted to be with them because it seemed a bit far-fetched, making the intentional choosing all that more apparent.

We never beseeched our pastor who married us to say certain words or give a particular sermon on our wedding day, so it came fresh to my ears when he based our marriage sermon on the words: "I choose you." Before he emphasized how Eric and I were choosing each other, he pointed to how God chooses us. Even though I strived to be someone that God might deem a perfect fit, I always fell short. And yet He chose me. He gave me the longing to be chosen, and then he gave me the gift of being chosen. We are an unlikely pair, but this makes our relationship all the sweeter.

My husband, Eric, has also made me feel chosen. The not-so-young girl who never dated a man more than four months was swept away by a man who had been married for over ten years and had three children. I didn't feel like I knew his waters at all, but he invited me in. He is four years older than I, so we never walked the high school hallways together, but he did have a locker in Jock Hall at one time. If we had been there together, I would have been intimidated by him for sure. His bedhead hair, strong build, and playful chuckle would have folded me up. Yet here we are after being together for more than fourteen years, and he is the one who has unfurled my shoulders and lifted my head.

As Pastor Dave said that day, "It is I *choose* you." It is not "I chose you." The choosing we were doing at the altar was not something to consider in the past tense, something completed and wholly finished once we said our vows and walked back up that aisle. Choosing each other needed to be in the present tense, something we would always be in the process of doing. And when the circumstances make that choosing more unexpected or difficult, being chosen or choosing the other feels even more profound.

I wanted to have something engraved on Eric's wedding band before we were married, but I couldn't come up with something beyond putting our date on it. So, I opted to not have anything engraved. I kept it a clean canvas. However, after our ceremony, I knew what would press against his finger and line the inside of his ring. "I choose you."

Because we all simply want to be chosen.

Chapter 2

Great Expectations

I was seven and a half months pregnant when I decided to finally begin reading Charles Dickens' novel *Great Expectations*. It seemed so appropriate since I was expecting and also had such great expectations. Plus, I loved his other novel *A Tale of Two Cities*; its ending is breathtaking and an all-time favorite of mine. As Sydney Carton sacrifices himself out of his love for Lucie, he says: "It is a far, far better thing I do than I have ever done, it is a far, far better place I go than I have ever been." I wanted motherhood to be a far, far better thing than I could ever imagine...I was enamored with those words "far, far better." And I longed to know what such sacrifice and love could look like in my own tale. How could I be a modern-day Sydney Carton to my own light, Lukas, as Sydney had been to his light, Lucie?

There I was a month later reading *Great Expectations* one Sunday night, looking at the 100 pages left to complete before my due date, merely two weeks away. So I burrowed into bed eager to see if all of the characters' unmet expectations were soon to be realized. In the midst of my darting eyes and determined pace, I felt my thighs strangely dripping with water. I had noticed that pregnancy seemed to be filled with "what the hell was that?" moments. Could it really be my water breaking? It didn't feel momentous enough.

But a quick phone call to my doctor confirmed my water did break, and I would be delivering the next day. I set the novel aside, disappointed that my expectation of finishing it before Lukas' arrival would remain unmet. However, I had new expectations to tend to. Since tonight would be our last night of uninterrupted sleep, I curled up closer to Eric and relished the silence. I cradled my bulging stomach, which would morph yet again tomorrow; I wordlessly said goodbye to this season of parenting a child inside me; and then I glanced at the baby crib next to me and tried to imagine Lukas lying there. Which features would look like Eric? Which might look like me?

In the midst of my revelry, Eric turned to me, after drinking over a bottle of wine earlier on our porch, and said, "I hope I feel all right tomorrow." *You?!* I thought. *Aren't you supposed to be worried about how I might feel tomorrow?* He didn't stop there. He added that he had changed his mind about Lukas' middle name, and we needed to find a new one. *Really? The night before his birth you spring this on me?* It took us months just to come up with our son's first name; we certainly didn't have it in us to decide upon a middle name in merely one day. This wasn't how I pictured it.

I wondered whether preparing to give birth was difficult because I didn't know what to expect or because I expected too much? I wasn't sure; I imagine it was both. I only knew that my expectations were getting jostled right when I deeply needed them to feel steady.

The next day brought more of the same as expectations continued to go awry. One expectation I had for our delivery day was to intentionally capture key moments as if my eyes were taking snapshots of the day. I knew this went back to one of my college professors telling us she decided against having a wedding photographer. She explained to our class that she didn't want to rely on someone else's eyes. If they went without a photographer, she reasoned they would pay more attention to those fleeting moments. And so I had hoped to adopt this mindset for Lukas' birth day.

However, I failed to acknowledge a remarkable difference between a wedding day and a delivery day…namely, the pain! Because of the great pain delivery holds, my eyes were most often squinted shut. Breathing was all I could concentrate on. One of the nurses commanded, "You need to sit up; we are giving you an epidural." Yet I continued to just lie there. No amount of reprimanding was going to motivate me since I was trying my best to remain in a self-made cocoon. My hope was to shrink my outside world as the world inside of me kept magnifying and demanding more. I envisioned my womb filled with strong tentacles that were wringing and clutching my insides. Despite my non-compliance, somehow the nurses wrangled me into an upright position, and the epidural encouraged those tentacles to settle down and rest.

With such relief, I asked who was doing the delivering that day. I knew it was unlikely I would get my preferred doctor, but I had met most of his colleagues and I was happy to hear it would be another favorite. However, when the time came for me to push, the nurses were unable to locate her. She had turned her pager off to get some sleep and forgot to turn it back on. So instead, I had a stranger peek between my knees and quickly introduce herself, "Hi, I am Dr. Moran, and I will be helping you deliver your baby today." I didn't have time to be disappointed or think about it much, but I also couldn't help but notice that it wasn't even going as the staff had anticipated.

I shut my eyes yet again, but this time I followed whatever the nurses told me: I pushed, I breathed, I counted, I pushed some more. And then finally I settled down and rested: Lukas was beside me. They laid him on my chest with his hands sweetly folded. Eric drew near, too, and interlaced his fingers with mine. Immediately my outside world was far more compelling than my inside world. At last, this moment was as I expected.

Even in a sterile environment, with beeping machines and medical strangers witnessing what feels so private, I relished the moment's unique beauty. My eyes blinked: once, twice, more times than I could count. I was busy taking those mental snapshots my professor had recommended.

Then all too soon hands lurched into my camera's viewfinder as they abruptly scooped Lukas up and carried him to the nearby incubator. Eric would later tell me that it was then that he noticed a flurry of doctors and nurses gathering around Lukas, who was scoring very low on his APGAR tests amidst other medical concerns. Someone asked me if I had taken an amniocentesis test, which should have alerted me to their concern, but I was innocently savoring my ice chips. And, more importantly, I was savoring that Lukas, the unseen, was now Lukas, the seen.

This revelry was also pierced: "Lukas needs to be transferred to Children's Memorial Hospital as we suspect he may have a detached aorta. There are some indicators suggesting Lukas may have Down syndrome, but we will need to run a blood test before anything is confirmed." The atmosphere of celebration suddenly became hushed and thick with concern. I watched all of the faces around me fall. My mother, who earlier that day tried to make me laugh as we walked through the halls, was now biting her lower lip and fidgeting with her hands. My dad looked frozen. And Eric wasn't making eye contact with me.

Later Eric would tell me he was shrinking his outside world in order to process all of the logistics the upcoming weeks would hold. But in the moment, I could only replay yesterday's conversation as he drank that bottle of wine. We dreamed of living overseas and introducing our son to a wide range of people and cultures. This potential news was dashing his newly birthed dream, and I felt responsible.

Almost as quickly as people flooded our room, they began to vanish. The doctors and nurses were busy tending to Lukas on a different floor. My parents made their way back to their hotel to give me and Eric a chance to talk. And then Eric made his way out the door to give his mother a ride home.

It felt so unexpected to be left alone. I laid in my bed and tried to process the day. What did I know about Down syndrome? I could only think of one boy from our church who had it. He was often draped across his mother's lap on a bench outside the sanctuary. *Was he always tired? Lazy? Overly attached to his mom?* I remember everyone thought he was very sweet even though I watched most people keep their distance. I was so young that I never understood why this school boy talked like a toddler nor why his tongue seemed too big for his mouth.

This little information I had did not serve me as I contemplated what a possible diagnosis would mean. I only knew it wasn't part of my great expectations. When these thoughts became too overwhelming, I would force myself to go back to name hunting. We still had a middle name to decide upon, which now felt like a welcome distraction.

And then around 2 a.m. the phone rang. "We are about to transfer Lukas. Would you like to come down to say goodbye?" The answer that sprung to mind was not the one I said aloud.

"Sure. I will be right there."

I expected my motherly instincts to emerge right away and reveal my desire to show sacrificial love...the kind Sydney Carton had taught me. But instead, I simply wanted to burrow into my hospital bed and read a novel with a much different name.

I took my cramping, wiggly body to the nearest elevator and made my way without the wheelchair or nurse I had on my earlier visit to Lukas. Ultimately, this visit was rather uneventful. I merely kissed his forehead and whispered "goodnight." It was all I could muster as I felt watched and unsteady. I needed Eric beside me. These were not snapshots I wanted to take or remember, so I rather quickly began the trip back to my room. But as I stood in the elevator, I realized I didn't know where my room was. My eyes had been closed so much that day that I never saw a room number.

And here was the final blow. When I returned to my floor, the front desk was empty. No one was there to let me back in. I held back tears as I imagined myself sleeping on the hallway's floor in a hospital nightgown. No room, no bed, no dignity.

Very little fit with my expectations of the day. I had heard too many mothers talk glowingly of their children's birth stories. I wanted my son to have such a beginning, too. But then I remembered a mom whose story also had some unexpected twists. I wondered if Mary felt disappointed on the night her son was born? Did she imagine herself nestled in a bed with her child on her chest? Did she shed any tears when she had to lay Jesus down on harsh, crunchy straw? Did the smell of a stable and the crowd of animals fit what she envisioned for her son's first night in this world?

Did she have to grapple with the stark difference between what she imagined and what God provided? Or, did she already know that the far, far better place was worth all of the moments that fell short of her expectations? This night was far worse than I imagined. Those words of "far, far better" would have to wait.

For now, I had a small flame to cup my hands around and protect.

Chapter 3

This Little Light of Mine

When we were looking to name our son, it was important to me his name held a significant meaning.

I liked the name Dmitri, but it meant "follower of Demeter," the goddess of grain and agriculture, which wasn't compelling to me. Meanwhile, my husband liked the name Gordon, but it reminded me too much of the Spanish word "gordo," which means fat. I already knew how hard that label was during my adolescent years, let alone giving my son that name at birth. Although we both liked the name Jacob, it meant "usurper" and frankly that just made us nervous!

And so we lingered without a name. We just called him what his three-year-old cousin named him: Buzz. For surely Buzz Lightyear was the perfect name for any growing boy. Then on a car ride in Traverse City, Michigan we came upon his name...Luke.

Not only was this the name of my favorite gospel in the Bible, but it also meant *Light* or *Bringer of Light*. As a woman who believed she would never bear her own child, of course this baby was going to bring me unimaginable light. He would displace the shadow that had hovered over the name of mother, the name I thought I would never hear.

In the hospital I began singing to Luke his theme song: "This Little Light of Mine." It was a song I learned in Sunday school and particularly loved for the accompanying hand gestures. It was fun to wave my pointer finger in the air as we sang "This little light of mine, I'm gonna let it shine." All of those who now wave lighters at rock concerts owe something to this childhood song. Even more than this finger waving, I really loved the part when we "[hid] it under a bushel" and then screamed "NO!" allowing that finger to flourish all the more.

When I sang to Lukas in his hospital room, I treasured the reminder that I needed "to let him shine." He would shine in ways far different from Buzz Lightyear, but he would shine nonetheless. And I have often had to heed the words of "hide him under a bushel...NO!" because there are many moments when it is so much easier to hide. It is easier to leave Lukas at home instead of taking him to the grocery store where he once threw a rotisserie chicken out of the cart and spilled juice all over their floor. (Side note: I shoved it back into the container, bought it, and served it for dinner that night.) It is easier to forgo attending the theater where Lukas may blurt out sounds at inappropriate times, throwing lots of unwanted attention on us. In general, it is easier to limit his contact with the outside world where things can quickly go awry. There are so many insidious ways we can be tempted to hide these precious loved ones. Hide them in order to protect them. Hide them in order to protect ourselves.

But if his light is going to shine, then I have to allow him to flourish like that finger which waves even higher after it has been wrongfully covered up or potentially snuffed out— "don't let anyone blow it out...NO!"

I named him Luke because names are important to me. And so not only has he been named to shine forth his light, but I, too, have a role to play. I need to prevent those bushels from hiding him or those winds from blowing him out.

Part II

Hide Him

places of hiding,
a hidden path, an unknowing

"Faith includes noticing the mess,
the emptiness and discomfort,
and letting it be there until some light returns."
— Anne Lamott

Chapter 4

Nouns First

There was a phrase I heard quite a bit after Lukas was born: "He's a Downs kid." I have since learned there is a better way to say this: "He is a child with Down syndrome." We all are children before we should have any other label attached to us; otherwise, we can become too easy to dehumanize, pigeonhole, or stereotype. If we put the adjective first, that is what our language asks us to meet first, and I think we always want to meet the person, the noun, first. I like the idea of beginning with nouns and then adding helpful adjectives, if needed.

I was so thankful to see Lukas' face before hearing his diagnosis. He simply was my son, with hands folded, eyes closed, and a blue nightcap on. He was all that I had waited for. It wasn't until days later when I officially learned he had an extra chromosome. Until then, I cherished the opportunity to process all of the awe woven into childbirth before I had to process any fear or grief.

However, soon after our hospital stay, I entered a season when he was more of the adjective than the noun to me. In those first months after bringing him home, I remember seeing his Down syndrome every time I gazed at him. It shouted louder than any other noun, attribute, or characteristic. I, too, was falling prey to giving him the label "Downs kid."

I wondered when I went to the grocery store if I needed to address his Down syndrome diagnosis with strangers. Surely they saw it as clearly as I did, and I questioned whether they deserved some explanation. When I went to the park and put him in the Baby Bjorn facing me, I worried that people might think I was trying to hide him. *Was I trying to hide him?* When I paged through a book called *Gifts*, which is filled with photographs of babies with Down syndrome, I tried to see each child and not just the markers associated with this extra chromosome. My thoughts were consumed by his diagnosis.

But then a woman at our local Gigi's Playhouse (an organization dedicated to helping people with Down syndrome) gave me words of hope: "You probably see his Down syndrome the most right now, but soon that will fade away and you will just see Lukas when you look at his face."

And that is exactly what happened. He went from being my Downs child to my son with Down syndrome. From being a Downs kid who had the name of Lukas to Lukas who had Down syndrome, just one of his many characteristics. This was a critical shift.

Years later Lukas' grandfather, Papa Joe, said: "I don't think Lukas looks like he has Down syndrome." Yet Lukas has many of the characteristics that reveal this diagnosis. It is just that once love steps in, labels fade away.

Chapter 5

Manna for the Day

I remember dreading the moment I would hand Lukas over to the doctors. The base notes were those of a last goodbye. He was so small, which left so little room for error, and the clean canvas of his chest would return to me scarred. Since Lukas' birth, we knew he would need heart surgery, but it felt all too soon as he was only three and a half months old when his scheduled day arrived.

The weeks prior to this cold, December morning I found myself plagued by unshakeable worry and fear. *How do I prepare my heart for this day? How will I feel when I place Lukas in the nurse's arms, knowing the surgeon would soon be cutting his chest open? How will I handle the hours of not knowing spent in a waiting room?* The questions tumbled in my mind like laundry in a dryer.

When my Bible study teacher asked me how I was doing, my eyes welled up and I said, "Not good. I know I don't have what I need for that day."

She replied, "Of course you don't." And then she gently smiled.

"Can I tell you something?" she went on. "I want you to think about how God interacted with Moses and the Israelites when they were in the desert. Did He give them all kinds of food beforehand and let them portion it out?"

I shook my head. "No," she continued, "He gave them the exact amount of manna they needed for each day."

"He does the same thing today, you know. He hasn't given you the strength for that day because you don't need it yet. He gives us 'our daily bread' -- our manna for the day."

I kept mulling over those words: "manna for the day." They released me somehow. I didn't have to figure out how I was going to conjure up the strength myself since God would be the one to provide it.

It was still dark the morning we piled into a cab and headed to the hospital. It felt good to be done with the waiting and finally embarking on the doing. I made sure I didn't hold Lukas too tightly. I was aware of my desire to envelop him, perhaps in a strange attempt to return him to life inside of me. It was safer for him then. Now that he was on the outside, we were much more aware of the many complications that could arise. So in this moment, I just focused on being gentle.

Once we arrived at the hospital, all of our attention went to the paperwork involved with registering Lukas. This allowed me to escape into my head, that inside place which felt safer for me, too. I simply kept taking the next small step: sharing my insurance card, walking to the hospital room, meeting the many doctors, changing Lukas into surgery clothes, rocking him gently. But before long, that big step arrived. The nurses came in and said, "We are ready for Lukas." I allowed myself to take a deep breath. In all of my imaginings, I suspected this moment would be dramatic, so I was surprised when it turned out to be rather calm and understated. I kissed Lukas and handed him over with a simple: "Take care of him." I think those might be the words God whispers over each new baby He places in parents' hands. There it was...the moment I feared most being infused with a strange peace: manna for the day.

As I pondered what I should do during the difficult waiting hours, I knew my mind would struggle to read a book. No need in reading the same page over and over. I wanted something that could take my thoughts captive, yet not be too taxing. I landed on knitting. I wasn't very good at it, so it called for some concentration. Yet my hope was that its repetitive nature would lull me into a meditative state. It felt somehow symbolic for me to knit in the waiting room as the surgeons knit Lukas in the operating room. It was a strange way for me to join them in the task of weaving something together. It felt like another piece of manna.

There was still one more dreaded moment ahead of me—seeing Lukas post-surgery. About a month before this surgery, in an attempt to better prepare myself, I met with another mom whose daughter had the same atrioventricular (AV) canal operation Lukas would have. She brought pictures of what her daughter looked like post-surgery. Naively, all I expected to see was bandaging around her little girl's heart. However, there she was with her mouth taped into fish lips, pinned down by a large green breathing tube, and entangled in a host of purple wires. It was an image I desperately wanted to shake.

But instead of forgetting that image, I found myself revisiting it over and over again. Most of the time I put Lukas in the place where her daughter lay. I practiced envisioning the moment I would first see Lukas overwhelmed by such a sea of tubes and cords. I thought this might prepare me like the medical student who slowly becomes accustomed to witnessing gruesome scenes. However, when the time came, it still managed to take my breath away: Lukas laid there paralyzed and entangled in so many man-made items that it was hard to find his soft flesh.

I knew there would be emotional waves throughout the day, I certainly wasn't asking God to make me steely, but I had hoped I would have enough manna for such tricky junctures. Since I couldn't reach out and touch my vulnerable baby, I reached for the scripture I had tucked away in my sweater pocket: "You will keep in perfect peace those whose minds are steadfast, because they trust in you." With my mind far from steadfast, I was acutely aware that perfect peace would continue to elude me. *I am struggling, God. I need more manna.*

And then it arrived. It was a surprise visit from my obstetrician – Dr. Moses. He is the doctor who I had hoped would deliver Lukas, but who had instead come this moment to deliver me. I know you might not believe this, but my doctor of over fifteen years has the last name of Moses. There was Moses in the Hebrew scriptures who experienced firsthand what it was like to rely on manna every day, and there was Dr. Moses who was the manna I needed on this very specific day. He stood beside me and bore witness to the beauty that Lukas was healed; he had made it through surgery. He gently reminded me, "The tubes and wires will fade away, but Lukas' mended heart will remain." There was perfect peace in such words.

Afterwards, I reflected on how my day shared a similarity with the Israelites, the group of people Moses led out of Egypt, into the desert, and towards the Promised Land. My walking through one day of surgery glaringly pales to their forty years of wandering in the desert, but I caught a glimmer of what it feels like when we don't have much to hold onto. A desert makes us more aware of what we don't have rather than what we do have: limited water, sparse retreats from the sun, few distinct land markers. Likewise, I walked into Lukas' surgery more aware of what I didn't have: emotional strength, steadfast peace, or a knowable outcome.

Even so, that day helped shift my focus onto what I *did* have: God's provision when I needed it most. Lukas' scar points to so much more than a heart surgery. When I look at it now, it reminds me of when God graciously revealed that He still gives us manna for the day.

Chapter 6

Just Be Mom

During our time with Early Intervention (EI), the first three years of Lukas' life, our therapists did a wonderful job of imparting this organization's philosophy. Their goal was to model ways of teaching the child so the parent could continue those lessons throughout the week. Parents were to be active members of their children's growth. Somehow Lukas' progress each week felt like a report card on me. Had I practiced enough with him during the week for him to improve? Just holding Lukas in my arms and watching Sesame Street felt indulgent. My mind kept reminding me - *you could be working on something right now.* Blowing bubbles wasn't for fun, it was to help him learn how to purse his lips. Going down a slide wasn't for fun, it was to help him gain strength as he climbed the ladder. Sadly, fun was always at the service of gaining ground.

I felt like we were in a race of sorts, but Lukas and I weren't at the starting line with everyone else. We were about three miles back, starting at a deficit. We had considerable ground to make up, so strolling or taking a water break felt negligent. Consequently, the idea of merely relaxing with Lukas always stirred those "not enough" voices. *You haven't worked with him enough this week, so go in the other room and try some more. He needs a mom that will fight for him at every turn, so get up and work some more*. Exhausting "not enough" voices.

If everything was going to be harder for him and require more time and repetition, then my charge was to spend our time doing just that. Repeating the skills as often as possible. Walking upstairs and ensuring he alternated his feet, learning the sign language for animals and action words, threading wooden blocks with a shoe string, to name just a few of our current lesson plans.

Then one day our physical therapist, Dawn, said: "You have to take time to just be a mom, too. Enjoy Lukas."

Strange how hard it was to hear those words.

Those words felt like a sure path towards failure. How would we ever close the gap if I eased up on his "training"? The others would continue to gain ground and soon we wouldn't even be able to see the group ahead.

Around that time, I went to a conference and learned that it wasn't about making up the gap. The gap would always be there. My sense that EI was a vehicle to give Lukas a head start in order to close the gap was misguided. EI was there to support his growth and help him meet milestones, but the gap would remain. In fact, the gap would increase as Lukas became older. It was very evident that I needed to find a way to embrace the gap rather than rally against it.

But this all led to me learning an even more important lesson: I needed to embrace that it was ok for me to just be mom. Working with Lukas on all of these skills placed me in the role of his coach or tutor. There was a striving rather than an abiding energy about me. I was the arms that pushed him more than the arms that comforted or enfolded him.

At various times in my life, my mom has been my tutor or teacher. One year she taught a summer workshop class at our local dance studio. In order to illustrate a point, she shared a personal story about me. As others laughed, I withered. I vividly remember how difficult it was to have my mom as a teacher. I felt the shift as she left my side and instead took her place across from me. Since then she has played many roles in my life, but most of the time I just want her to be my mom.

I think that is how Lukas must feel, too.

Yes, I will continue to help him with homework and the various therapy skills he needs to practice; but through it all, I am carrying Dawn's words with me.

The image of life being a race has never been helpful to me. Why did I ever think that it would be helpful to my son? He is a young boy in his own lane just looking for a personal best. Like all of us. Not a race, just a journey. And rather than being the one holding a whistle or a stopwatch, I want to have my arms free to embrace him.

I want to just be Mom.

Chapter 7

The Lurking Monster

As life sped ahead, I was slow to notice a growing trend. When I was home with Lukas, I fully delighted in him. I relished his teardrop eyes, his expansive smile, his bedhead hair, and his overall charm. I imagine that is not surprising. Of course a mother finds her child winsome. However, that was not always the case.

There were times upon leaving the house to join other moms and children that I wondered where the beauty in Lukas' face had gone? What happened to the eyes that captured my heart only hours ago? Why did his forehead suddenly seem so long? Why did his uttering "Ma ma ma" and "Da da da" now seem insufficient, even though I praised it in the kitchen this morning?

I want to love him in public like I love him in the living room.

Yet there is a monster that lurks in public places that doesn't live in our home. It is the monster of comparisons. When Lukas is the only one around, he is incomparable. We cherish everything about him. But once he enters a space that is populated with other children his age, he doesn't seem to measure up. He isn't walking like the others or stringing words together. He isn't fully feeding himself or holding his weight when we carry him.

Images of a race surfaced again. None of this bothered

me in the sanctuary of our home and yet once the sanctuary was gone, I felt bombarded by the arrows of competition. "My child is doing _____;" "my child is ranked _____."

And then I stopped to ask myself what was really important? *Are comparisons healthy? Don't they always lead to a winning versus losing mentality?* When I compare my figure to models or my intelligence to scientists, I certainly don't measure up. So instead, the temptation is to pick out people who make me feel better about myself…at their expense. This game inherently leads to a trampling on others.

What happened to building one another up because we want ALL of us to be strong, to feel worthy, to succeed? Entering into this dangerous world of comparisons isn't healthy. We are charged, as parents, to guide our children and prepare them, but our mission doesn't include tearing down "the competition."

I love what Ann Voskamp says, "We aren't here to one-up one another, but to help one another up."

Lukas reminds me that my role is not only to build him up, but to build up all of the children in my midst. To love him in public like I love him in the living room because doing so allows the world of comparisons to fade away.

Chapter 8

IEP and the Slipping Banner

Individualized Education Program (IEP) meetings seem thick and daunting to the newcomer, and we were about to embark on our first one. We had heard many stories of how parents had to fight for their children at these meetings, some hiring advocates to join them on their child's behalf. Consequently, we wanted to walk into this gathering feeling prepared and clear about Lukas' needs. I always loved the process of interviewing for a new job because it pushed me to reflect on my personal goals. This IEP meeting felt a bit like that—it encouraged us to consider our lifelong goals for Lukas. We knew these desires might change over time, but from our current vantage point, we had two educational goals: 1) Lukas would explore ways to discover and better know himself and 2) he would become a vital part of his community, learning how to engage as a contributing member.

In preparation for this meeting, I asked the Special Education Department Chair at my current high school for her advice. She said, "I often want to nudge the parents under the table so they ask for more services. I can't take the initiative on some things, so I wish they would. Don't be afraid to ask for what you need."

This should have given me the wings I needed to walk into our conference with a confident boldness, but it didn't. After being a teacher for over twelve years at that time, I had attended enough IEPs to know how delicate they could be. If the parents asked for too much, grumblings might arise once they left: "They are being completely unrealistic in their requests." "Their child isn't the only student we have to shepherd; we can't possibly fulfill all of their demands." The boldness of these parents often worked against their child as the team felt less inclined to pour themselves out on the student's behalf.

This put me into a bit of a bind. Do I listen to this leader and trusted colleague who suggested we "ask big" and forge forward with great expectations? We all know that when students are held to higher standards, they exhibit more growth. Or, do I listen to that teacher voice whispering in my ear as well? The one that said, "Watch your tone." Boldness can sometimes sound like brashness. Proclaiming "You need to provide these services for our son," could easily feel like a wagging finger, one that would just make those around the table shrink or feel a bit defiant.

I had witnessed the magic of "we" too many times to not put that word at the tip of my tongue. "Do it" needed to be "We want to join you and we hope you want to join us." The shift from "You" to "We" gently paved the way for greater morale among the team. After such meetings, we all dispersed with an eagerness to collaborate and truly help the student and family.

Hmmm...what was I left with? High standards with a Big dose of unity. We were about to see how this would all play out. I had spent years trying to put myself in the parents' shoes at these meetings, leaning in to better understand what they were going through, and now I was truly in those shoes.

Prior to our meeting, we were given a hefty document to read through—a compilation of Lukas' teachers' and therapists' observations and recommendations. Eric and I spent considerable time wading through all of their notes and highlighting those places for further conversation. Lukas had been in a self-contained kindergarten class for the past year and only included with his peers for lunch and music. Consequently, our goal was to discuss how and when they would move Lukas into a classroom with his peers.

In his present classroom, our greatest concern was that his classmates weren't helping him improve his social and communication skills, nor was he helping them. In fact, we knew they were all exchanging many unhelpful behaviors and very few words. Lukas was barely verbalizing at the time and he wasn't in a room that lent itself to him hearing others talk. It would be like me going to Mexico to learn Spanish, but hanging out in the library where no one uttered a word. Just as I would want to move out of that library, we knew Lukas needed to move out of that self-contained classroom.

Meanwhile, we witnessed how he would try new things and say new words after time with his cousins. As they played, he would hear lots of language, and they would unknowingly teach him needed social skills, like sharing toys and taking turns. For example, I spent a summer urging him to ride his big wheel to no avail. But when his cousin came over and jumped on one, he now had a more enticing incentive to ride one himself. She was a much more effective teacher than I was, and we knew Lukas' classmates had the potential to be powerful teachers as well. We didn't want him to miss out on that gift.

When trying to pinpoint how this transition from a self-contained classroom into an inclusive classroom would go, one of the teachers said, "I can best explain through an analogy. Placing Lukas in a typical classroom right now would be like throwing him into the deep end of a pool. He could too easily drown. Instead, we believe in starting children in the shallow water where they can better focus on the basics. Then when their skill set has improved, we transition them into those deeper waters. That is our model for Lukas' education right now. It is hard for us to predict when he will be ready for an inclusive classroom. All we can say is that the deep end is our goal."

I knew firsthand the importance of shallow waters; Lukas and I had spent lots of time learning how to be patient there. In many ways, her analogy made sense. Yet these shallow waters sounded more like an eddy that kept circling in place rather than an entryway to deeper waters. When we inquired more, they fumbled to give us any concrete examples of how this had worked with other children.

Since Lukas will not live in a world separated from others upon graduation, we wanted his education to be a training ground for the inclusive world he would face. If he was going to become a good member of his community, a goal we had already established, we suspected those lessons would be hard to learn if he was tucked away in a far-off room. He needed to experience being a full member of his classroom, not just a visitor his classmates experienced when he peeked in for lunch or PE.

We had learned through research that placing a special education student in a classroom not only benefits the child with special needs, but also *all* of the students. The typically developing students' test results go up, often because they are given opportunities to help teach the special needs students. But perhaps more importantly, the students grow in empathy. Eric brought up these studies and their data, and the Director said, "I have seen that research. I don't believe it."

Our vision for Lukas was not matching up. I imagined someone kicking me under the table urging us to ask for more; however, in that meeting, it felt like the wrong fight. I thought about emphasizing our desire to work with them, making sure they heard "We" come out of my mouth as often as I could utter it, but our philosophies were so different. *Was this a place to compromise? Or, was this a place to hold onto convictions?* We wanted to persevere and pave the way for others as we had watched other parents do; but, for us, in this season, we needed to find another way.

There we were at this first IEP meeting with our "High standards and a Big dose of unity" banner falling down on both sides. They weren't believing Lukas could thrive with higher standards and we weren't finding unity with their philosophy.

After the director said her final words of not believing an inclusive model brings out the best in All children, Eric looked at me and attempted to calmly close his notebook. He was done. Not just with this meeting, but with this school district. The very same district we had both attended as children and held dear.

It was hard to start this journey with such a dim light. Since we were at the very beginning of Lukas' education, we didn't want to fight our way through the many years that lie ahead. We yearned for something beyond the Us vs. Them model. We yearned for We. With ground that seemed nonporous, it was time to find a different place where we all could grow.

Chapter 9

For Nothing Is Impossible with God

I have found that sometimes I am drawn to a phrase even when I don't entirely understand it. The claim "nothing is impossible with God" is one of those phrases for me. It is comforting, even when it feels far-fetched. It somehow plucks me out of a world that can make me a skeptic, a realist, or at least someone who is painfully aware of life's limitations and disappointments. And instead, it lands me in the possibility that there could be more. That what feels out of reach is perhaps possible. Not surprisingly, I have clung to these words when things have felt impossible for Lukas.

Since my curiosity about this claim kept deepening, I decided to learn more about it. I found this phrase, "For nothing is impossible with God," in the Gospel of Luke. It is placed at the beginning of Luke's writing as if to set the stage for what is to come.

So, let's see. What *is* impossible in this story?

God taking on human flesh seems impossible. As I yearn to have a God who surpasses my humanness, it seems unexpected that He would bring deity to us in the form of a human. Wouldn't that just make me susceptible to finding other people worth my idolatry? And what about God dying at the hands of men? That should be impossible. Men shouldn't be able to take down the Sacred so easily nor would I expect God to allow it. Jesus' birth and death are both shrouded in impossibilities, not to mention His resurrection.

Then there is Elizabeth, Mary's cousin, who was around 60 years old and barren, yet she suddenly found herself with a heartbeat pounding underneath her own. And Jesus' mother, Mary, who had not known intimacy with a man, yet she suddenly conceived a child. In just these two women, we witness the range of how God can do the impossible.

Right before our move from Crystal Lake to Southwest Florida, I lounged on a blanket and listened to a Kenny Rogers' concert alongside one of my dearest friends. She gently asked me how I was feeling since our hope to adopt was no longer possible. After years of waiting, we only had one week left on our adoption contract; our time had come to an end. I could only feebly tell her I was thankful we tried. We had heard many times how hard it was to adopt these days, nearly impossible.

The next day our family gathered to help us finish packing and purging things we would no longer need, namely winter clothes and baby toys. We then pulled away from the home that birthed Eric and me in our marriage, helped us grow roots as a blended family, and served as our training ground for raising Lukas. We were only a few hours into our drive when we received a call from our adoption agency. "If you can fly to Texas by the end of the week, a new family member awaits you. Her name is Sarah."

The circumstances weren't as romantic as I had pictured. Her possible birth into our family was revealed in a cross-country car ride. The invitation came to us in a front seat strewn with empty wrappers, half-used water bottles, and Steely Dan playing in the background (Eric gets the shout out for that one!). Lukas' birth veered from what I imagined and now Sarah's did as well. God seems to show up not only at the most unexpected times, but in the most unexpected places.

Somedays I can hardly believe that God has intervened in people's lives as told in the Bible. Did He really part the Red Sea? Did He really feed 5,000 people with just a few loaves of bread? Did He really give two women, Elizabeth and Mary, the children of their dreams?

But I find it even harder, most days, to believe that He still does the impossible in our midst. Life can seem so ordinary. All of us just trying to get by on what is possible that day. And then I am reminded of one more woman who was given a child of her dreams. Not once, but twice. Lukas, who continually reveals how the impossible becomes possible, and Sarah, who reminds me that God can resurrect lifeless ashes.

I still don't fully understand this phrase.

And yet...I somehow know it to be true.

Chapter 10

At the Core

When we met Sarah, who was three months old, we were eager to know every inch of her. The whites of her eyes mesmerized me as they seemed to glow. I gazed hard to learn if she had dimples (they seemed to be hiding in her cheeks somewhere). And her long fingers captured my attention as they looked like the batons of a conductor. However, when we brought her back to our hotel room, I discovered something unique about her that we didn't catch upon our first encounter.

In the middle of her precious stomach, that perfect place to bury one's lips and blow raspberries, was a protruding belly button. An appendage of sorts. It stuck out about an inch, fleshy, but stiff, with a slight pinkish tint. Perfect for a small game of ring tossing. We would later learn this is not so unusual, just a herniated belly button; however, I put her in onesies to hide this protrusion. It gave me pause before diving down to smother her tummy in kisses. And more than anything, it summoned me to reflect on this part of our body.

Why did it bother me so? This was something the pediatrician said would go away within a few months. Yet I live in symbols...they mean more to me than most people...and so I searched for deeper meaning. What was this extended belly button trying to teach me?

I started with a simple free association. The first thing that came to mind was how our belly buttons remind us that we all start connected to our mothers. It was the tunnel bringing us nourishment. Since Sarah is adopted, I wondered if this malformed belly button was a symbolical reminder that I wasn't the womb who carried her. I didn't get to provide her that initial sustenance. We didn't start connected and so her belly button looked different in order to somehow reflect that.

But that wasn't it. I may not have been the womb to nurture her from the darkness into the light, but I am the arms and heart that have held her since. Her unique belly button wasn't there to make me ache; it was there to illuminate. To eventually bring me more light.

Simply put, I believe our belly button is an important mark God has given us. It is our reminder that we came from someone. He could have put our belly button anywhere on our body, but He put it where we all can see it: He placed it at our core. The only body part we have that was distinctly connected to another is at the center of who we are. Perhaps God wanted to give us a daily reminder that connecting is at the core of life, it is at the core of being human.

Connectedness is God's heartbeat, too. He could have thrived independently, but He chose to live alongside Jesus and the Holy Spirit. He knows how community brings life and nourishment, so He has modeled this for us all along.

Now when I look at my belly button, I am reminded of our longing to connect. We need cords that link us to others. When we were in our mother's womb, we needed that cord so our bodies could be saturated with nourishment. And as children and adults, we still need cords of connectedness because they are life-giving to our souls.

God has yet again shown me how He redeems. This belly button that I once tried to cover up is now so beautiful to me, much like the heart surgery scar on Lukas' chest. Through Sarah, God reminds me that we receive a tremendous gift when we are connected to others.

Chapter 11

The Bubble

When I was pregnant, my doctors were very upfront about all of the complications that could arise due to my increased age: spina bifida, Down syndrome, preeclampsia, gestational diabetes. But my greatest fear was having a child with autism. I had heard it was more common in boys and firstborns...and our firstborn was going to be a boy. We knew a handful of people who had a child on the spectrum, and out of Eric's eight college housemates three of them had children with autism spectrum disorder (ASD).

This diagnosis scared me more than others because I knew so little about it. My meek understanding was that it meant my child would not want to connect with me, would avoid eye contact, and would be squirmy anytime I initiated affection. I knew John Travolta had a son with autism, and I pictured his son living in a bubble of sorts, isolated from everyone. It was only later that I remembered John Travolta was in a movie entitled *The Boy in the Plastic Bubble*. My mind had strangely conflated autism with this movie, leaving me with a very limited and inaccurate picture of autism.

I remember going to a Down syndrome convention and seeing "Dual diagnosis" as one of the sessions. I pondered what it would be like to contend with multiple diagnoses...as if one wasn't enough. Then I gladly crossed off this session as I tried to narrow down which workshop I would attend.

Although this topic was crossed off in my convention workbook, it was not crossed off in our journey ahead. Lukas was about five years old when someone first recommended we test him for ASD. She referenced his frequent arm flapping. Since Lukas loved eye contact and was very affectionate, I naively doubted Lukas had autism, but followed her advice anyway. The test was simply the neurologist observing him for an extended time. Afterwards, I bluntly started the conversation: "Is Lukas on the spectrum?"

He replied, "Yes." His bluntness far exceeded mine. My face revealed my befuddlement and disbelief. As he noticed my surprise, he continued by saying, "I think we are all on the spectrum."

This last statement made me sigh with relief. *So, he doesn't really have it,* I thought. It allowed the possibility of this diagnosis to retreat back into the shadows.

However, three years later a behavior therapist in Florida brought the subject up again. She noticed some of Lukas' idiosyncrasies and questioned if there was another diagnosis impacting him. Her first thought was obsessive compulsive disorder (OCD). This was not surprising to hear as we were well acquainted with his obsession around shutting cabinets and drawers, turning lights off, and clearing any space in front of him. She thought we would be wise to have him tested again.

I dreaded more testing. But when I heard the difference of services granted to children with autism compared to those with Down syndrome, I started to wonder if the diagnosis I had long feared might just be the glimmer of light we needed. So I called a friend who has four daughters, two of whom have Down syndrome. Her youngest daughter had recently received a dual diagnosis.

"How did you figure this out?" I asked.

She said, "If it weren't for the fact that my older daughter presented so much differently than my younger daughter, Kylie, I would have thought all of Kylie's behaviors were due to Down syndrome."

However, since she saw a distinct difference in her daughters, she had Kylie tested and learned she had ASD. I now knew someone who would attend that dual diagnosis session I had crossed off in my convention workbook. And from talking to her, I was pretty sure I would be joining her as a future attendee as well.

As my spirit protested another label affixed to Lukas, another set of difficulties he would have to face, another host of limitations, my friend's words quieted me. "You need to rethink how you are approaching this label. The behaviors in our children are there with or without the diagnosis. The child does not change. But the label carries important power for children and our families. They can now receive the services they desperately need. The label has helped Kylie not hurt her."

I couldn't believe I was going into this new testing *hoping* Lukas would receive an ASD diagnosis. I had previously associated this new label as more harm to my son, but I was beginning to see that it could bring great help to him.

And so it did. We went from receiving two hours of behavior therapy a week, paid out of pocket, to receiving fourteen hours a week, covered by insurance. These extra hours of training made such a difference for Lukas. Yes, the label was helping, not hurting.

Furthermore, it not only helped him, but it helped us as well. We now could have more understanding when he screamed in terror at the dentist or barber shop or shuddered at fireworks—it was a sensory issue for him. We now could understand his more limited palate when it came to toys or games and thus lay down the "let's branch out" battle we kept having with him. We could now understand why he talked in a unique voice, or why he had to sit in the same seat every night at dinner. These were all part of him having ASD.

Ultimately, I was the one in the bubble, not knowing enough about autism and how it impacts people. I think ASD makes Lukas more rigid, but I also think it gives him a great sense of humor. It makes him more limited with toys, but it also helps him beat me and Eric at memory games. It may be another label, narrowly defining who he is, but it is also the very thing that is expanding his opportunities.

Neither of us could live in a bubble any longer.

Chapter 12

Pull up a Chair

Lukas loves to sing and does a darn good rendition of "Jesus Loves Me This I Know" and "Amazing Grace." However, we don't bring him to the worship portion of our church service like the other kids his age; instead, we bring him right to the room that is designated for him and his teacher.

The people who care for Lukas at our church are lovely—they pour themselves into this little boy. Ms. Lorraine, who is in her 70's, does not shy away from caring for him even though his physicality could quickly overwhelm her and her weakened knee. She is living proof that we are never too old to step into unknown waters. And his other teacher, Ms. Robin, who is his special education teacher at school, could easily desire a break or a Sabbath from him on Sundays, but instead she chooses to find even more time to nurture him and model for others how to interact with him. Their love is stunning. It is the love of pursuing that lone sheep.

So it may seem like we don't bring Lukas to worship in order to extend his time with these special women, which is partly true; however, there is another underlying reason we keep him out of the sanctuary: we don't want him to disturb the congregation.

It is similar to why we bring Lukas for haircuts right before the salon closes. We know people go to the beauty parlor to be pampered, so Lukas' cries of fear upon hearing the clippers would disrupt this soothing atmosphere. And we know people go to church to seek serenity, so Lukas' outbursts would disrupt this meditative atmosphere.

It is our fault that he can easily go unnoticed on Sunday mornings as he is in his own private room. And what has recently struck me is this: What if Lukas is part of God's message?

God teaches us to welcome the broken, the outsider, the lonely, the one who looks different from us. And Lukas is one of these people. Yet *we* aren't even inviting him in. And if his parents don't invite him in, how can we expect others to do so?

In a New Testament story, an owner of a house prepared a banquet and invited many guests. When the banquet's date arrived, he sent his servant to gather those who had been invited. However, the invited guests all passed on this invitation. They were too busy, too involved, or too dismissive to set time aside for his special gathering. And so this master, a figure meant to represent God, tells his servant: "Go out quickly into the streets and alleys of the town and bring in the poor, the crippled, the blind and the lame." Those on the outside were the ones invited inside.

Lukas is a child this servant would have found on that street.

If God wants us to be quick to remember the forgotten, then I need to make sure Lukas isn't tucked away in a room where he can be forgotten. Lukas may be part of Sunday's message. A quiet call to invite him in. An opportunity to remind us all that we can't delight in God's words that we are fearfully and wonderfully made, but then quickly cross off the kinds of people we don't think fit that definition.

We ALL have been invited to the banquet table. Whether we come or have an excuse that keeps us from God's lavish love...each day will tell. But we need to make sure we don't become the ones handing out the invitations—welcoming some while tossing other invitees to the side. God is the designated host.

So, let us call out into the streets, alleys, and country lanes to welcome those who may feel forgotten. Then let us get them a chair to pull up to God's banquet table—He has already invited them to the feast.

Chapter 13

A Double Life

I live a double life. There, I said it. And it is true. I live one way when the kids are around and an entirely different way when they are gone.

When they are home, our house is on what we call "lockdown." All technology is stored away in hard-to-reach cabinets: remotes, cell phones, reading nooks, etc. We have $800 worth of locks in place to ensure the kids can't escape and the keys for the locks are hidden away in drawers or cabinets. Our refrigerator is locked and then roped together with the freezer below it. The Keurig is unplugged because Lukas is newly infatuated with making coffee, the kind that spills all over the floor.

However, when our children leave for school, the remote comes out and proudly rests on the kitchen island. My phone is finally available to me and I can respond to the plethora of messages that have gone unanswered. The doors open up for fresh air. And Eric and I allow our breath to hit a deeper place within us. That inner tremor that comes with living at such a high vigilance subsides. Eric wears a watch that tracks his stress, so he can show me how the bright orange becomes blue once our children leave. I don't dare purchase one of those watches. I think just seeing my stress level depicted in color would cause it to rise!

Now you may think I am the kind who is quick to overreact, but if that is true, it is not unfounded as we have had a kitchen fire, two police visits, and one Department of Children and Family Services (DCFS) visit due to some of Lukas' actions. But I get ahead of myself.

The most recent mishap took place on an unassuming Saturday morning. Eric was headed to Tampa with Sarah to see our grandson play baseball while Lukas and I remained for his horseback riding lesson. They left around 6:00 am, and I just wasn't ready to start my day. So, I put the television on in hopes of encouraging Lukas to cuddle with me on the couch for a while.

Instead, he kept asking me to "come here." I didn't move, wordlessly rejecting his request. I relished the quiet. Certainly, he would soon join me in the family room. But Lukas was determined to get his way. He wanted me in the kitchen and he concocted a sure plan to lure me there.

As I gently closed my eyes, I started to smell something. I couldn't place the stench. Burning rubber? It didn't make sense. My lethargy on the couch was stripped away as I noticed a slight fog in the kitchen. I scurried into the room and spotted the flames in our microwave. What??!!! There was some inedible substance on the microwave tray causing orange flames to wave and rise. Lukas wanted me in the kitchen and his plan worked! He put my reading nook in the microwave, pushed the convenient thirty seconds button, and successfully had my nook aflame.

LUKAAAAAS! NO!! DANGER!!! HOLY _____!!! This was all after a recent lesson from our behavior therapists on how children with Down syndrome feed off of our emotional outbursts. They reminded Eric and me how funny we all can look when we are angry. Our emotions won't dissuade Lukas from negative behavior; in fact, they tend to encourage him to pursue more antics in hopes of seeing such a "rain dance" again. So, our behavior therapists coached us to remain calm and use few words when Lukas was non-compliant.

Well, I certainly hadn't mastered that lesson yet. I was more like Rumpelstiltskin after the princess guesses his name. Feet stomping, bug eyed, screeching out my words. Deep fear fueling it all. He could have been burned, the house could have caught on fire, my imagination painted this scenario in all kinds of dark ways...all because he wanted my attention and I wanted rest.

Rest became even more elusive after this incident. How would I sleep now knowing the damage Lukas could do in the middle of the night? That evening I slept on that same couch...the one I was begging to give me just a few more moments of calm. Now I was begging this couch to keep me from a deep sleep because I wanted to hear any strange noises or smell any unusual smells. Lukas was no stranger to those couches in the middle of the night, so I feared he would come down and wreak more havoc.

Thus, we now have two belts that secure our microwave, each with a code to keep Lukas from opening them. And we have a bungee cord that wraps from our microwave handle to our stove handle so they both are secured and unable to be opened. This mishap caused us to increase our lockdown measures.

However, I am more afraid of what can happen to Lukas outside our home. The week we moved into our new house we noticed the funky lock on the front door. We could unlock the door from the inside, but if we didn't push the button on the side of the door, it would remain locked. It was just a matter of time before I forgot to push that button, closed the door behind me, and realized the keys were inside. We often left the house in a scramble, which was fodder for me locking us out. Thus, we arranged for a locksmith to fix this door. He did a preliminary visit on Thursday, I accidentally locked me and the kids out of the house on Friday (a whole other story!), and so Saturday I decided to leave the door unlocked. I couldn't imagine asking our babysitter's dad to come hijack our sliding glass door again to help us back inside. Our locksmith was coming on Monday, so I just had to make it two more days without new locks.

That Saturday morning, I hustled to unpack boxes while the kids played. Their new game was to knock Eric's guitar case down and pretend it was a balance beam. So when I heard a bang, I assumed that was the noise. I was on a roll with my unpacking, loving my Stevie Wonder tunes, and ready to impress Eric with all I would accomplish before his return.

Then I noticed something.

It was very quiet. I couldn't hear the kids playing. I ran down the stairs, calling their names, and continued to hear nothing. After weaving into each room, I discovered they were nowhere to be found.

That is when I remembered I had left the front door unlocked. We were so used to having all our doors bolted I forgot this new two-day arrangement. The sound I heard wasn't a guitar case falling to the floor, it was the front door slamming shut behind my escapee children.

Immediately startled, I sprung out into the street (pretty sure I was still wearing my pajamas). However, that was nothing compared to Lukas. He was galloping naked, smack dab in the middle of the road, while Sarah tried to keep up in her footies. Ah, this was how we were going to introduce ourselves to our new neighbors! I saw a man on his cellphone, so I quickly introduced myself as their mother. Notice how I didn't say "proudly introduced myself." The first neighbor I would meet looked startled and told me he was speaking to a police officer; the cops were on their way. We already had a police record due to a previous escape by Lukas, so I dreaded explaining myself again. Another neighbor reminded me that alligators lurked in nearby ponds and I shouldn't let my kids run around unattended.

Within minutes, there was a police officer at our door ready to investigate the situation. I think our recent past was making this new experience all the more haunting.

At our previous home, we had the biggest scare to date. We had just finished a weekend of hosting our friends from Belgium when we decided to take a family nap. This was very rare for us, but entertaining and a long day at the beach had wiped us out. Lukas fell asleep on the couch, so I joined him there while Eric and Sarah each went to their beds. When I awoke, maybe an hour later, Lukas was gone and the front door was wide open.

We scrambled to make a plan: I would jump into the car and scour the neighborhood, while Eric would remain close in hopes of Lukas' return. I drove very slowly so I could scan for Lukas, which helped keep my emotions and breathing calm. I longed to see his bright blue sneakers, but then froze as I imagined them floating on one of the nearby ponds. When I was maybe six homes away from ours, I saw a police car in a neighbor's driveway. This had to mean something, but rather than pull over to ask for help, I drove right by. I knew if they had bad news for me, I would need Eric by my side.

Then right by our driveway another police car sat. The cop asked: "Are you Mom?" I didn't know what answering "yes" would mean. What news might await me? I barely nodded my head. He replied, "We have your son." Breath hit that deeper place.

Eric jumped in and we followed the cop car. He led us to the neighbor's house, which had the other police car in its driveway. We then learned the story—Lukas had walked to this home, saw the garage was open, opened the garage door leading into their home, and joined the family on the couch. These neighbors were strangers to us, but they welcomed our son. After deeply thanking them, and eager to process our emotions in private, the police officer said, "I will need to follow you back home to ask further questions."

Once we were back in the car, we realized that Sarah was still up in her crib! We had been using a "tent" on her bed (it kept her from crawling out at night), so we knew she was still safe there, but we also knew that leaving the home without her wasn't going to look good. We didn't have any excuse except for our steely focus on Lukas.

Our fears were for naught, as we had an amiable conversation with the police officer. He ultimately told us we would most likely receive a visit from DCFS since it was standard procedure. And, indeed, the following day a card was on our doorstep from one of their employees. It said: "Call me when you return." She would arrive within a half hour.

As we scrambled to clean our home, some serious disagreements arose. Do we tell her we had two bottles of wine with our guests or say it was only one? Do we change Sarah's messy dress or leave it on? Was our goal authenticity or ensuring we were above reproach? *Does a messy outfit really call us into question*? I thought. Yet Eric didn't want to give this officer any reason to doubt the care we gave our children.

When she arrived, there were few formalities, just an impending interrogation. Eric bravely went first and later told me their conversation was fine. I felt a bit more scrutinized. When she learned my father had been in the army, she said: "That must have been difficult having such a demanding father." I had never made any reference to his actions as a father, nor would I describe my dad in this way, so I could tell she was fishing for any wayward fact.

The culminating event was a drug test. We had to urinate in front of her to ensure we didn't slyly slip someone else's urine into the vial. There I crouched while her shadow loomed over me, a fitting image of our relationship. Before leaving, she said, "I remember losing my child one day at the mall. It was scary." I wanted to ask her if she had someone from DCFS come and visit her because of it? Admittedly, I was feeling bristly. But families that have children with special needs can use more grace than others, not less.

I heard that having a child with Down syndrome sometimes feels like playing the game of Whack a Mole — as soon as you "whack down" one behavior, something new pops up. This part of the journey has been tiresome. It would be dishonest to skip over those places that continue to ache and have heaviness to them. They are there. They are the shadow to the light. They are perhaps what causes us in the Down syndrome community to bond together so quickly as we all have our own horror stories that only have levity in hindsight.

As soon as we prevented Lukas from one dangerous behavior, he discovered a new one. However, Lukas' desire to slip through a door and run away has been constant. So on that morning of unpacking, I shouldn't have been surprised he was running down another new street. He was probably off to meet more neighbors and, unknowingly, garner more attention from the police. It is easy to feel like a criminal when your child keeps you in close connection with the cops! Although this second encounter was less serious than the first, it threw me back into feeling watched and inept.

Even though we had a rocky start, our neighborhood has shown us the beauty of stepping outside our home. Sheila, a marvelous neighbor in her 90's, routinely welcomes Lukas as he waltzes right into her home without a knock or notice. He loves playing on her "old-fashioned" phone. She was quick to tell us she had a brother with Down syndrome, so Lukas must have intuitively known where open arms awaited him. One afternoon we delivered homemade Christmas cookies to our neighbors. We were touched by how many of them welcomed us inside and were gracious as Lukas zigzagged around hunting for phones. We are continually reminded that when we walk out our front door, fear can arise, but meaningful connections can also await.

I often wonder what living in a state of lockdown does to one's psyche? To have things closed off, barred, confined, unavailable. To try to lock my children away in a safe tower, making sure the dangers of the outside world are kept at bay. Safety comes at a cost, no question. When we escape the difficulties of the outside world, we also miss out on its beauty. Lukas' song pricks at me: "Hide him under a bushel...NO!"

The physical lockdown is one thing. But it is the

emotional lockdown I worry about more. In hopes of not being embarrassed again, how am I shutting myself away, confining myself to a very limited area? How am I keeping us small when all I really want is for us to grow and enlarge? How am I allowing our past to eclipse what we can be in our future? These all seem like very important questions to ask myself. I know I can't let safety usurp our desire to take major steps in this world.

We may have to remain in a physical lockdown, but we will always need to fight against an emotional one. The kind where we long to take risks and expose our children to all that is around them, but instead we stay nestled in our home for fear of something going awry. The kind where we desire to introduce our children to all kinds of people, but then only bring them into circles we know will accept them. The kind where we believe the greatest danger is unlocked doors, when really the greatest danger is not finding enough doors to go through.

We may always have to live a double life when it comes to our physical world, locking things up when the kids are home and releasing them once they are gone. But I think if we aren't intentional this could easily seep over into us living a double life emotionally.

That is a double life I am not willing to live.

Chapter 14

Silent Speaking

Someone asked me the other day, "What has been the hardest aspect of raising Lukas?"

My answer came quite easily, "Not fully knowing his heart and thoughts." His limited communication colors any difficult moment with more tension and lament.

When he cries and says, "owwie," he can't tell me where the pain is coming from. How do you help when you can't determine if it is a headache, stomachache, toothache, etc.? We point to different body parts and ask, "Does it hurt here?" But he just shakes his head no.

When he bursts into tears, seemingly out of the blue, I have no way of understanding his sorrow. "Lukas, what is making you sad?" But, so far, he has not been able to give me an answer. Ultimately, he has no pressure valve to release his emotions, so they just stay bungled and layered inside.

I know when my heart is heavy with pain, I crave a listening ear. I just need to release those stored-up emotions so they don't creep out sideways. Lukas needs to do the same, but he doesn't have the words to do so. Instead, he has to physicalize his communication: desperate taps, yanking on arms, all kinds of frustration and unacceptable behavior is born out of his inability to communicate with words. He remains voiceless when it is clear he is aching to tell us something.

I know the ache of that state, of feeling silenced in moments when emotions are piling up. However, those have been rare moments for me while they have been the norm for Lukas. He remains voiceless and unable to invite others in, and so there he is trapped within himself. Virginia Woolf once said, "I thought how unpleasant it is to be locked out and I thought how it is worse perhaps to be locked in."

We all deserve to have our voices heard and our hearts listened to. And Lukas, so far, has not been given that luxury.

Consequently, I have been praying that God would set Lukas' tongue free like He did for Zechariah. In the book of Luke, we learn Zechariah didn't believe the angel who came bearing unimaginable news: his wife, Elizabeth, would bear a child in her old age. As a result of his unbelief, Zechariah was muted. Yet once their son was born, "his tongue was loosed and he began to speak, praising God."

This story buoys me with hope.

Not long ago, I attended an event at our local church to hear a recommended guest speaker. At the end of her talk, she invited anyone that was interested to come forward and receive prayer. I decided to do so.

She had penetrating eyes and quickly recognized my fatigue. As she stood beside me, she asked God to give me the ability to pray without ceasing, just as the Holy Spirit does on our behalf. She wanted me to have the fire of the Holy Spirit. That sounded like the kind of energy I could use!

"Have you received the gift of speaking in tongues?" she asked.

"I haven't," I nervously replied.

So she started wiggling my chin and tapping my jaw as she prayed that my tongue would be loosed and set free. That all those thoughts that I had not been able to utter to God would be unleashed and voiced in a new burst of language. That words would spill out of me in ways I had not experienced before.

I yearned for such a gift. I tried to pray the same for myself, echoing in my heart whatever I heard her say aloud. She even encouraged me to just start talking...to see what might come out of my mouth. But I was mute. I couldn't find any words. My heart felt full of things to say, but I remained silent and unable to grasp her hope for me.

I identified with Lukas.

As I pray over him and beseech God to free his tongue and unleash his language, he mostly remains quiet...a boy of few words.

We aren't all given the same gifts. I never received the gift of speaking in tongues and Lukas hasn't received the gift of free and full language. I maybe can't communicate to God in tongues, and Lukas can't communicate to me in full sentences, but we still work on leaning in to hear those unspoken words. To bypass words so we can hear each other's hearts.

Nevertheless, Lukas remains a mystery to me.

I used to love teaching stories shrouded in ambiguity, those that kept full knowing out of reach. They were rich soil for discussions. But I think ambiguity is much harder to live out. We crave certainty in its stead. We want answers, not all of the questions. Yet God's very nature is full of mystery...there is so much about Him that is unknowable. And He continues to teach me to sit in the unknowing.

That doesn't always feel comfortable, just like not knowing Lukas more fully doesn't feel comfortable. But I am learning to listen to the silence. Even when nothing is uttered—something is being said.

Chapter 15

Special Needs Indeed

"Hello, everybody, so glad to see you," sings Ms. Katie as she rocks and strums her guitar. From dancing with scarves, magically blowing out the lights, and animating a parachute, my children love the *Music Together* classes we attend. As I find a place in the circle, I gaze at the mothers around me, sometimes noticing their unique outfits or their hip hairstyles, but mostly admiring their calm. I observe their behavior to uncover what it is that makes their children sit so serenely in their laps. I admire their effortless poise.

Meanwhile, my two children prance around the room either pulling on noses or pulling off glasses. As I rush to rescue the dad donning a baseball cap currently enduring Lukas' stranglehold, Sarah darts off to strum a guitar she is not supposed to touch. I do not have any poise. Instead, I have a sweaty upper lip and a growing agitation.

The end result is that I just want to stay home, protected, and away from any potentially judging eyes. "Hide him under a bushel...No!" The volume of Lukas' theme song dims in my heart during moments like these. My two hands are not enough to wrangle my children in, and my feet trip over themselves as I assess who to grab first. Everyone can see I need extra help with my children, but that dependency makes me feel broken and ready to hide.

In her stunning book *The Broken Way*, Ann Voskamp laments her own brokenness, but her husband, The Farmer, shares what the fields have taught him:

> "The seed breaks to give us the wheat. The soil breaks to give us the crop, the sky breaks to give us the rain, the wheat breaks to give us the bread. And the bread breaks to give us the feast. There was once even an alabaster jar that broke to give Him all the glory...Never be afraid of being a broken thing."

I could see from his examples that brokenness always led to something greater. Instead of setting my eyes on what felt cracked within me, I needed to shift my focus to what it yielded, the abundance born out of my need.

I started by thinking about Lukas' neediness. My battle cry is to never let him see dependency as an occasion for shame. I want to encourage him to engage with the world in the midst of his needs. Yet there I was wanting to run and hide when my own needs confronted me.

God suggests a better way. Our needs are not an *occasion to escape* other people, but an *opportunity to engage* with other people.

My hope as a mother is to help Lukas see that he may have to rely on others, but that is part of the beauty found in his story. To be a "special needs" child is not a label of failure, it is rather an invitation to build a community around him. To choose to see onlooking eyes as empathetic. To truly see our need as something that brings out the best in others and even the best in us.

I may not be the mother in the circle that is refined and still, but I am the mother who is spurred to connect with more people. I meet the dad wearing the baseball hat, have extended conversations with the teacher, and thank the mom who helped me chase down one of my kids. The Farmer is right; abundance awaits us. Our needs are weaving our lives together so we can experience deeper community.

I can't tell Lukas I see the beauty in his needs unless I am willing to start seeing that beauty in my own. I have special needs, indeed!

Part III

Blow Him Out

feeling tossed about, losing footing,
experiencing the windstorms

"The deeper that sorrow carves into your being, the
more joy you can contain. Is not the cup that holds
your wine the very cup that was burned in the
potter's oven? And is not the lute that soothes your
spirit, the very wood that was hollowed with
knives? When you are joyous, look deep into your
heart and you shall find it is only that which has
given you sorrow that is giving you joy. When you
are sorrowful look again in your heart, and you shall
see in truth that you are weeping for that which has
been your delight."

— Kahlil Gibran

Chapter 16

Re-member

Just the other day my Mom and I reminisced about our love for repetition. Re-reading a book or re-watching a movie offers new gifts each time. We found David Letterman's use of repetition humorous and part of his charm, so we typically chose his show for our late-night viewing. And since we both have a theatrical background, we were good at pretending to hear any revisited story as if for the first time. We felt at home with repetition.

But my love for hearing stories over and over took a slight turn when my Mor Mor (Swedish for mother's mother) started slipping into dementia. Now instead of repetition feeling familiar, it felt threatening.

My Mor Mor used to say, "Did I have anything *on* my head? I know I don't have anything *in* my head." I watched this as a young woman in my 20's and usually found my Mor Mor to be whimsical and funny. But my Mom watched this descent up close and felt the pangs that came when my Mor Mor talked about how her daughter never visited...even as my Mom sat right beside her listening to those very words. I was learning that dementia and Alzheimer's could usher in a host of pain.

When Lukas was not even three months old, I returned

from a doctor's visit and went online to look up a term he mentioned. In that search, I learned that Dr. Potter and his colleagues at the Florida Alzheimer's Disease Research Center, stated that "By age 30 to 40, all people with Down syndrome develop the same brain pathology seen in Alzheimer's disease, including a nerve-killing buildup of sticky amyloid protein clumps. This contributes to accelerated nerve cell loss and dementia." A later search revealed that Michael Rafii, Associate Professor of Clinical Neurology at USC, found that "by the age of 40, 100 percent of all individuals with Down syndrome have the pathology of Alzheimer's in their brain."

Words such as these snatched my breath away. The guilt can run deep. I was still struggling through the role I played in causing Lukas to be born with Down syndrome, and now I had to contend with another future battle I may have inflicted on him. My chromosome that *forgot* to split was eventually going to launch him into a state of forgetting. I could only hope that we would walk this Alzheimer's path together, so I wouldn't have to lucidly watch his descent.

As I digested this new information, I nursed Lukas in his rocking chair. This helpless boy would become helpless again way too soon. Tears escaped my eyes. The future felt like a wilderness of panic. I was losing my breath, that which nourished me, and I was losing my milk, that which nourished Lukas. All I could do was experience feeling stuck even as I rocked back and forth.

Many moments later I heard Eric coming upstairs after his day at work. He would be greeted by my tears. With so many moments of tears in those early days, I imagined they were becoming wearisome to him. Even though I tried to brush them aside, he noticed. "What is wrong?" he asked. When I told him, he was quick to remind me that in forty years there could be many medical advancements. "We are not going to get ahead of ourselves. We will just honor the present and see what technology brings."

Against my better judgement, I returned to the internet. What steps *was* science taking in its Alzheimer's research? A study in San Diego was using people with Down syndrome to better understand this disease. "In the general population, there's no good way to know who is going to develop Alzheimer's. But for people with Down syndrome, it's a near certainty," said William Mobley, chairman of the neuroscience department at UCSD. So, the hope was that people with Down syndrome could help the medical field unlock some of the Alzheimer mysteries, leading to more efficacious treatments.

Although I know this interconnectedness should have encouraged me, I couldn't help but flashback to when I directed the play *Flowers for Algernon*, based on Daniel Keyes' novel. The story traces Charlie Gordon, a 32-year-old man who is developmentally delayed. He is given the groundbreaking opportunity to undergo a surgical treatment that would greatly increase his mental capabilities. The scientists had already tested this procedure on a mouse, Algernon, and this mouse had flourished, so they felt confident it would also help Charlie. And, in fact, it did. Charlie became a genius. One of the characters, Professor Nemur, says that they had "taken one of nature's mistakes and by [their] new techniques created a superior human being." However, his "getting smart" didn't make his life better. In many ways, it made it worse. Eventually he regressed back to his former state of mind and science's claim of helping humanity ended up crushing Charlie.

Just thinking about this play was evoking all kinds of turmoil within me. I wanted to sit across from Charlie and tell him that his worth was not dependent on his intellect. He was as worthy before surgery as he was after surgery. He was not one of "nature's mistakes." I guess that is the same message I want to say to Lukas and all our children—your worth is not connected to your intellect, your appearance, or your abilities. Your soul lies much deeper than any of these and this is where your precious worth is found.

Our children are not people to fix, just like Charlie was not a young man to fix. They are not the ones that need adjusting. We are looking in the wrong place when we try to change them and not our own misperceptions. They remind us to assign worth "just because." Not because of any hierarchy or human achievement scale. Not because we measure ourselves against one another. Not because of things that are fleeting: memory, beauty, abilities. We are loved "just because."

I also shuddered at the thought that perhaps our children are the Algernons in these Alzheimer's studies. Were they being used like Algernon, a trial run for those who followed? The ones that really mattered? The "real" people? To put it bluntly, were our children lab rats? This connection between the San Diego study and the play was beyond unsettling to me. Yes, I wanted to help people battling Alzheimer's, I saw its ravaging effects on my Mor Mor and more people since, but not at the expense of people with Down syndrome. We can't value one group above another. I think that is how we are supposed to feel about *every* discrimination. When we find those places where one group of people eclipses another, we need to shine light back on those faces who are falling into the shadows.

People with Down syndrome are a gift. Not because they are a gift to the medical field and those who can potentially be spared Alzheimer's. They are a gift "just because." Once that point was clear for me, only then could I turn and be reminded that we are all connected: the nursing child who already has the genes that lead to Alzheimer's and the 82-year-old woman who waned because of this disease. We are given the charge to remember each other; we just need to do so with dignity and a clear sense that our worth was there before we ever arrived on the scene.

Chapter 17

Walls Won't Win

Lukas wasn't even a year old when I decided to join a Mothers of Preschoolers group (MOPS) in our hometown. In some ways, the diagnosis of Down syndrome slipped me into an isolated space. I think I subconsciously took on a feeling of being ostracized in order to experience the world I suspected lay ahead for Lukas; I knew it was just a matter of time before he was on the outside looking in. So, after this period of isolation, I was eager to experience a community around me.

Our first activity at this mom's group was to go around the table and share a lesson our child had taught us. After briefly talking about Lukas' Down syndrome diagnosis, I immediately went to the days leading up to Lukas' open-heart surgery. Doctors told us to look for signs of heart failure; we were actually supposed to welcome his shortness of breath, change in skin color, or swelling ankles and eyelids. I shared how throughout this time I was gripped by fear. But in the midst of it all, God planted a simple question in my heart: "Fear or faith?" At each moment, that was the question I needed to ask myself. Fear eats away at our faith; however, faith emboldens us to face our greatest fears. I concluded by saying that Lukas had taught me to keep coming back to this choice: Fear or faith?

The mom who shared after me told the story of how the doctors thought her daughter had Down syndrome. However, she knew her daughter didn't have it: "My daughter didn't look like that. We all know what they look like." Her lesson was about trusting her mother's intuition because she was right...her daughter didn't have Down syndrome.

She finished her story with a flourish, a happily-ever-after tone. Yet there I sat with a tightening throat and tears just waiting for a safe space. *Didn't she just hear my story of Lukas and my heartache? How could she say such hurtful words right in front of me?* "Her daughter didn't look like *that*." I came to this circle for a chance to connect and I left feeling more isolated than before. The sting was this—the church community was the first place I felt rejected and they were the last place I thought would make me feel this way.

I drove home letting my tears spill forth. This was not the community I needed. I resolved to not go back—it just didn't feel safe for my heart to do so. But as I saw my husband unexpectedly pull his car in front of mine on our town's main drag, I called to warn him of the puffy eyes and aching heart he would soon encounter in our drive way. I sputtered the story out with many stops and starts, just needing him to hear the anger I had that someone would treat Lukas that unkindly. To criticize Lukas and people with Down syndrome for looking "like that."

It was then that Eric told me we needed to decide how we would handle future incidents. He said, "We will be given many opportunities that can either drag us down or lift others up. Yes, we may hurt, but we can still help. We will either allow our emotions to build more walls or we will use our words to help tear down those walls." We needed to commit to seeing painful moments as teachable moments, for us and for others. We were just beginning to learn what life was like with Lukas, and we needed to invite others in. How could we expect others to know what we didn't know until we met Lukas? How would we learn to lean in with love even when the moments became rife with heartache?

Did that mean I needed to go back to MOPS the next week? Was that my way of making sure a wall wasn't erected? Honestly, I didn't want to; however, Eric's words urged me anyway. It was a simple act of choosing to stay in the circle. Of letting faith overrule my fear. Of giving wounds a chance to heal.

This MOPS group assigned everyone to a table so we gathered with the same women each week. Thus, I had to return and see the face that hurt me; I had to sit beside her again. We didn't become friends from that group, but over the year, we did get a better glimpse into the life of each other's child. The victory is that the conversation didn't end after that first day. We were given the chance to scratch away at a wall that didn't belong.

About six years later, I was reminded yet again of how walls can quickly erect. We were now living in Florida, and I was at Lukas' soccer game. He was having such a great time running around, off the soccer field, mind you! While his soccer game was taking place, he was more interested in a game of tag with another group of younger kids. This all delighted my heart until I took a closer look. They weren't tagging Lukas; they were chasing him so they could pull down his pants and show he was still wearing a pull-up. Lukas was full of laughter, not realizing their laughter was at his expense.

Full of concern, I made my way over to the young boy

with long, wispy hair who was heading up this game. "What is your name?" I asked.

After great hesitation, he finally said, "Mitch."

"My name is Mrs. Sanders; I am Lukas' mom. Can you tell me what you were doing?"

"We were pulling grass off of his shirt," he replied.

"No, you weren't. Please tell me what you were doing." He never did.

I wanted to have a moment of truth between us, but it was clear he wasn't going to confess, and it was clear my anger would increase if I pursued this conversation. I simply told him I knew what he was *really* doing and it wasn't kind. I walked away disheartened. Cruelty can start at such a young age; this boy was just in kindergarten.

The group of boys moved to another area of the field and were now running down a hill. Lukas followed them and again tried to join their activities. He remained blissfully unaware of their previous jaunts. I kept my distance in order to give Lukas some independence, yet my watchful eye remained. What was the game this time? It was tag again as they chased each other down the fast-sloping hill. But then I saw they weren't trying to tag Lukas; they were trying to push him. And it worked. Mitch pushed Lukas who fell to his face. This time I marched over to the young boys pulsing with anger. Eric's words made their way back into my head. Would my emotions build more walls or would I let my words tear down these walls?

"Hi, Mitch. What were you doing this time?"

"Just playing tag," he replied.

"Why did Lukas fall down?"

"I don't know."

"You don't know? Ok, I want you to know that I saw you push him. He clearly likes playing with you, yet you are not treating him well. I suspect you are a nice boy and that is what I would like to see. Here is what I ask: before I leave, I want to see you acting with kindness towards Lukas."

This time I think Lukas was aware that he was being mistreated. His body was more downcast and the laughter had subsided. I had no idea how Mitch might respond to my challenge of kindness; heck, I didn't even know if he *would* respond. But I knew that me towering over him with angry words would just be another form of bullying. Instead, I was to find ways to let walls fall down. The wall that said people with disabilities don't catch on to rude behavior so they are an easy target. That wall kept a distance between Lukas and the boys. And the wall that said I could use my role as an adult to power up over children. That wall kept a distance between me and the boys.

Maybe about thirty minutes later I looked over to the bottom of the hill, the very place where Lukas had been shoved to the ground. And there were three kids kicking the soccer ball to each other. The ball was making its way around the circle: Mitch kicking to Lukas, Lukas kicking to Aaron, and Aaron kicking it back to Mitch.

It was a beautiful image of kindness. I started with a circle of moms that made me feel isolated, and I ended with a circle of boys that made me feel restored: God's redemption.

Kindness kicked down the wall of ridicule that day because if we allow ourselves to walk back towards each other, walls won't win.

Chapter 18

Not Such Bright Horizons

As we walked in, a large fish tank greeted us. Bright magentas, forest greens, and vivid yellows. A great way to welcome people into this world of colors and life.

Lukas, four years old, had attended a Bright Horizons' daycare for the past year. They asked us to come talk with Lukas' teacher, Melanie, since new behaviors were emerging. Our goal was to brainstorm some ideas that would help both Lukas and his teacher. I suggested we schedule it after his parent-teacher conference at school, so I could bring in their ideas as well.

Consequently, I walked into this meeting jangling my own "fish tank." A new mini-carton of goldfish with five pennies attached by Velcro to its outside. If Lukas did five positive things, then he would receive one goldfish. Since his school had created this new reward system, I was eager to share it at our meeting.

As always, I was hopeful. After all, Melanie was very invested in our child: she helped him on the bus his very first day of school; she bought him his favorite book, *My Big Brother*, for Christmas; she rode with him in the ambulance the day he choked and stopped breathing. She had a precious history with him.

"We know today's meeting is going to be difficult for you," said Nancy, the director of Bright Horizons. And then Melanie began to list all of the positive growth she had seen in Lukas: more words, improved feeding skills, more activity on the playground.

And then Nancy took out her clipboard and presented us with another list: swiping the counters to clear them, falling out of his pack-n-play, throwing forks, grabbing food out of the garbage cans, standing on kids' toes, pushing kids, and requiring an additional hand during meals because of his past choking incident. It soon became clear she was making a case against him.

When do I bring out the goldfish and pennies to show them? When do I tell them he stands on my feet, too, in order to see the food I am preparing on the kitchen island? When do I tell them that he is probably pushing kids to get their attention since he has such limited language available to him? When do I tell them that this was supposed to be a meeting to find ways to help him, not a time to charge him with all of his wrong-doings?

However, I sat without words. There were cries of pain stuffed in my throat and if I dared to utter any words, I stood the chance that only those cries would burst forth. Better to remain silent.

Yet how could I be an advocate for my son in such self-imposed silence?

"I am sad," was all that I could utter. And then we were told that we had thirty days to find him a new pre-school. He was officially kicked out.

He was not welcomed anymore. Unwanted. A bad kid. All of these words swirled in my mind. He was being rejected from a place devoted to nurturing and supporting children. He was being tossed into the wind. If they could reject him so easily, then what would he face in his near future? What would await him on his next horizon?

I couldn't bear to know that my mere four-year-old was already being called "not good enough." That is a label time hits us all with, but at least I was spared this painful branding until middle school. Here Lukas encountered it before even entering kindergarten. By people who were paid to be kind. What would happen when he met people who weren't trained to help him? Weren't paid to show him compassion? Fear loomed before my eyes...and its stature felt overwhelming. I needed someone's feet to stand on; I needed to know that someone was underneath me.

Perhaps that was what Lukas craved in those moments he stood on my feet. Maybe it wasn't just about being able to see better, but also about knowing someone was there to provide him a sturdier foundation.

And there I was shaky and unable to establish my own foothold in this situation.

I was learning a lesson from one of my greatest teachers. We need feet to stand on. We need to know that someone is under us, buoying us to a height greater than the one we can achieve on our own. We need to know we don't stand alone in this world.

Thus, I welcomed him to put his feet upon mine...in hopes that together we might stand tall.

Chapter 19

Mirrored Pain

I was in the midst of teaching Albert Camus' novella, *The Stranger*, to my Advanced Placement literature class. We were discussing the significance of Meursault's lack of emotion at his Maman's funeral. How strange. How detached. How empty. We all confessed that we would feel quite differently at the death of our own mothers.

As I was driving home that evening, my husband asked if I had talked to my family. When I said I hadn't, he told me the news. My aunt had unexpectedly died while visiting family for Thanksgiving. I was taken aback, but not knowing how to process this information, I strangely changed the topic. "What are your plans for the evening?" I asked.

He replied, "For someone who is typically emotional, you seem very detached." And I was.

During class the next day, I relayed this experience to my students and shared how I now had a new understanding of Meursault. Since my students were very familiar with my emotional side, they seemed rather baffled when I told them I primarily felt numbed by this news. I anticipated attending a funeral where I would not shed tears. Perhaps a first for me.

As Eric and I gathered with family in the church's

entryway, we all began to reminisce about my aunt, retelling treasured stories. Although we knew grief was lurking all around us, laughter still managed to escape from our lips. This felt inappropriate for such a moment, so we quickly retreated into hushed tones and shy glances around the room. We couldn't figure out the dance between celebrating a loved one and honoring those in mourning. With a knowing glance, Eric signaled to me that it was time to enter the church's sanctuary.

As we tentatively stepped in, it wasn't the exquisite flowers or the ornamental windows that caught my attention, it was my Grandma sitting right next to her oldest son, the one who had just lost his wife of over forty years. Since he was in the midst of battling diabetes and kidney failure, his strength and mobility waned. There they sat side by side in their wheelchairs. He was my robust uncle, the prankster, the athlete, the treasured child. Yet there he was with sunken cheeks and frail limbs, skeletal and forlorn.

And then my tears came.

These were tears that needed privacy, where I could heave and wail and make those ugly crying noises without worrying about what others thought. I was totally unprepared. I had no Kleenex to wipe my soggy nose. I had no lozenge to busy my mouth and keep it from making gurgling gasps. I had no aisle to race down in order to find solace in a bathroom stall.

At least I was no longer empty. No longer detached.

"Why were you crying so uncontrollably?" my brother asked me after the service. My heaving did not go unnoticed. I had to ask myself the same question. And then it slowly became clear to me. My tears were about the image of mother and son sitting together in feebleness and frailty.

Yes, I grieved for my Grandmother having to watch her son in pain. Yes, I grieved for my cousins' and uncle's loss. But as I dug deeper, I realized that my real grief was for me and Lukas. Somehow, I saw us in this image of mother and son.

It seemed like in years to come I would be the mother sitting next to her shattered son. Lukas sitting there beaten down by life, physically weak and emotionally depleted. And me, witnessing Lukas in pain, yet unable to help him.

This seemed more tragic than death. In death I could release Lukas into God's care, those arms that have the ability to heal once and for all. But here, here I would continue to be too broken myself to help Lukas in his brokenness. I would sit confined by my humanness. My strength would wane and I would merely be able to sit by his side, as I witnessed my Grandma do with her son.

How does a mother bear watching her son in pain? Especially when she is not free to wrap him in her arms. Those clumsy wheelchairs stood in the way. How did Mary, Jesus' mom, do it? She, too, watched her son in pain and was unable to comfort him. The cross stood in the way.

And yet there was something beautiful in that image. A simplicity. No words, no gestures of affection, just sitting side by side. Breathing together. Finding comfort in one another's presence. A quiet love. A love that says I will be there for you even when there is nothing I can do.

We wordlessly say... *Here I am. I have come to sit beside you.*

Chapter 20

Hands Full or Handful?

There was a phrase I started hearing quite a bit. Whether I was with our children strolling through an art fair, playing games at a church function, or doing my weekly grocery shopping, someone would smile at me and simply utter, "You have your hands full." Although another mom may have heard this as an opportunity to bond over mothering young kids, I couldn't help but hear: "He is a handful." Like they felt sorry for me that I was dealt the troubling path of having Lukas. Like the gift God gave me was not a beautiful gift.

An old tape, one I had tried to erase, played in my head again: "He is too much and you are not enough." I wanted Lukas to be greeted with celebration rather than hesitation. Yes, gifts can be both difficult AND very good. Marriage is difficult and very good. And being Lukas' mom is difficult and very good. Maybe because these relationships are difficult, stretching, dare I say painful, they are all the more good. In their fragility, we instinctively know to treat them with great care.

I am a woman who had hands that were bare, open,

beseeching God for a child, and He filled them. So, yes, my hands are full.

If my hands are full, it is because God has filled them with abundance. Often with Lukas' young hand squirming to get away or Sarah's tiny hand yanking at me to carry her. Or sometimes it is with Lukas, curled into me, playing with my fingers while Sarah, on my other side, practices standing up by herself, grasping for my hand when she begins to wobble. My hands are carrying, caressing, guiding, grabbing, praying, and protecting. Yes, I am a woman with my hands full.

There are plenty of moments that feel overwhelming, but they also beckon me to reach for His hand. I am choosing to see these "handful moments" as an invitation to remember that my frailty finds rest in Him. It finds fullness in Him.

Now instead of sitting up at night concocting gracious responses to the next person who comments on my full hands ("Yes, they are filled in the best of ways" or "I love them being full"), I can simply say, "Thank you."

Thank you to God for the reminder that my once empty hands are now graced with little fingers and sticky palms. Thank you to those other moms who see me with compassion and remember how hard those early years with children can be. And thank you to my children for giving me "hands full."

Chapter 21

Training for Two

I felt like I was in a movie scene of sorts and the director just said, "Take four." But this wasn't four consecutive takes, these "takes" took place over a course of many years. The first call to "action" occurred when Lukas was four years old. I was teaching full-time then and his home day-care provider decided to start toilet training him. She posted board maker signs by each toilet, taught him the sign language for "potty," and had him progressing quite quickly. That was all until Disney World hit. We were going to celebrate my parents' 50th wedding anniversary, and I just couldn't take on toilet training in the midst of all the magic! So I put Lukas back in diapers for our days at the Kingdom. After that trip, he was no longer interested in toileting. The magic was gone.

The second time this fictitious director said "action" came when Lukas was six, right after I looked up how much it would cost to hire someone to toilet train Lukas. I read the amount, $1,000 a day, and was flabbergasted that anyone could charge this much. I told Eric I would pay myself that money once I trained Lukas. Now I was strangely looking forward to becoming a potty expert. Only one short week of work and I would have enough money for a long vacation!

I guess I was rather taken aback at how hard I found toilet training to be. Lukas would often dangle his feet into the toilet or pull the toilet paper into a huge wad on the ground, completely distracting himself from the task at hand. I would sit on a stool that bore Lukas' name and often find myself wiping stray urine off my lap. Meanwhile, Sarah had just learned to crawl, so her curiosity led her to join us in the small bathroom. Every time she joyfully barged in, Lukas shut down any toileting urge. Not only that, but every time we would celebrate his victory on the toilet, I would return to life outside the bathroom only to discover another accident he had minutes later. This cycle of victory to defeat was deflating. After about a week of trying to conquer this task, I told Eric I thought the professional potty trainers were cheap...a remarkable deal! And I placed our names on their waiting list.

We waited for a year and a half before our names made it to the top of the list. The third time we heard the words "action" came over winter break when Lukas was eight...a whole four years after our first try at potty training. We would extend our holiday trip of visiting family and friends in Crystal Lake, so these toilet trainers could work with Lukas. Their program was designed to train him in merely four days.

The long-awaited day arrived! The toilet experts set up shop in my parents' basement and were ready to share their expertise. Right before I left, I pulled out Lukas' puppets. I sang a quick song as if it were my pep speech before a football game or theater performance, and then I told them what a great motivator these puppets were for Lukas. When I leaned in to give him a kiss goodbye, he turned away and said, "Space please."

The lead trainer's face scrunched up; "Do you think it is

ok for him to treat you like that?" Of course I would like to see my child run into my arms and kiss me at every request, but that isn't the reality I live in. I explained to Helen how I taught him that brief phrase to try and curtail his habit of pushing me away when he wanted space. I wanted him to use his words instead. Judgement crept onto her face, but I silently reminded myself that I had to pick my battles; I couldn't counter him on all fronts.

Then I left. Around noon they texted and asked that I return by 2:00, two hours earlier than scheduled. I sensed something was wrong, but Eric tried to allay my fears. "Are they giving up on him already? It is only day one, Eric."

"No, sweetheart, they probably just want to show you what they have been teaching him," he replied.

As I stood at the top of the basement stairs, Helen said, "Do not smile at him or give him any praise; he has not been a good boy." I stiffened. I would need to greet Lukas in a detached, calculated manner, and I could feel the tension in the room. The day had not gone well.

Helen proceeded to tell me all of the difficulties they encountered. "Lukas' greatest motivator is control. Until that is broken, you aren't going to see any success." They were going to cancel the remaining toilet training.

Once she had listed all of the ways Lukas had failed, she then turned her attention to me. "I can see who has really been receiving the behavior therapy: You." Lukas was training me rather than me training him. She mocked my use of puppets. "Why wouldn't he want to misbehave? The pattern you have established is that he does something wrong and you bring out the puppets. Sounds pretty fun to me!" I could only think of *Sesame Street* and *Mr. Rogers' Neighborhood* and how they, too, used puppets to capture children's attention. Somewhere along the way I wasn't doing it right.

I kept peeking at Lukas who was in the room as she said such things about him and such things about me. His face had fallen. And the feelings of another failure came swooping in. I wasn't able to train him and now even the professionals weren't able to train him. Who could I possibly turn to next?

I had a difficult time ingesting any other pointers they were trying to give. My thoughts kept circling back to how Lukas and I didn't measure up. He was untrainable and I had been trained all wrong. I couldn't believe I was a grown adult and a fellow educator, yet I was unable to utter any response. I couldn't ask questions, probe for further help, or take any action to help make the day worth the financial and emotional toll. I had certainly lost my footing; I simply remained silent.

Meanwhile, they issued their last set of directions: "Wait until we leave, then put Lukas' diaper back on." This final action was a signal to my heart that we were back to square one. We had paid to learn that Lukas was too far out of reach, they were giving up on him, and I was responsible for creating this "monster"—my word, not theirs.

Somewhere in this process I noticed that "toilet" has the word "toil" in it. These words aren't linked etymologically, but I couldn't shake seeing the word "toil" every time I thought of toilet training. I looked up this word in the dictionary. It has two meanings: 1) something that binds, snares, entangles and 2) to labor continuously, work strenuously. Isn't that the truth? Yes, toilet training had been a snare, a web of failure entangling me, and it sure felt like strenuous work. Both definitions resonated.

Lukas and I now had three extra days up North without any plans. The whispers in my head said: "Stay small. Don't let anyone know about this toilet training debacle.

Huddle in and cocoon." But I had a small group of women in my life who were warriors against shame and they showed up at our door the following evening. They came so that this story could fall on soft soil. As I shared our experience, I saw their hearts quicken when I told them the difficult parts, and I saw their eyes soften when I expressed my sadness at letting Lukas down.

The gift was that I didn't need to hide. Our pain happened in the basement, but these friends were welcoming us back up the stairs. Eyes of judgement were being replaced with eyes of compassion. The voiceless woman of yesterday was being invited to find her voice in the telling of this tale.

The message we so often hear is that we need to carry our own burdens. Be independent and pull ourselves along. But what happened when Jesus had something heavy to carry? He shuffled along a dirt road, knees wobbling, face grimacing, barely able to take the next step. And there came Simon. Jesus did not carry His cross alone. Simon picked up part of the weight and they carried the cross together. This is what God wants our lives to look like. I love how God gave Jesus someone to help Him because He knew we would need a visual reminder to find others when we encounter our own dark places.

The evening ended with these women circling around me in prayer. The kind of cocoon God knows brings healing. My hands lay open-faced on my lap, simply a practice of surrender. And then I felt a hand place itself in mine.

When I slowly opened my eyes, I saw Lukas' small fingers intermingled with my own. Lukas and I had found others to help us carry this cross, and he wanted to join in such beauty.

Chapter 22

Abandon

"He needs to go." Those were the closing words from an aide at Lukas' school. Lukas was lethargic, croup-like, and pale. Yes, he needed to go home. But her words scratched against a very recent wound.

After being away visiting family for Christmas holiday, Lukas was out of the routine his therapies gave him. Even though he was having great success at horse therapy before Christmas, when we returned, he fought me to even put his helmet on. He then refused to get on his horse. The next week was more of the same. This perplexed me as I was so used to seeing Lukas' joy when his horse would trot. I knew he loved horseback riding, but now he was refusing what he used to treasure. At the end of his second unsuccessful lesson, his teacher came over and said, "If he doesn't get on the horse next week, we will need to put another child in his place. We have a long waiting list." Here is what I heard: "He has to go."

This came just two weeks after an even more painful day. That day of learning the toilet training specialists were going to discontinue their services for Lukas. He was too non-compliant. He was beyond their reach. In other words, "He has to go."

This wound of feeling left behind I suspect goes back to

the day of Lukas' birth. Everyone around me had the best of intentions, yet there I was all alone on a day I envisioned great unity. Into that hospital room, the ache of abandonment started to creep. I was birthed into a new role of caring for someone, but in that moment, I just desperately wanted others to care for me.

When I was younger, I had a very different reaction to the word "abandon." I craved this state of being. I yearned to dance with abandon, to release any self-consciousness so I could feel untethered and soar. And I loved when I had those moments of laughing with abandon. Lightness and delight. However, now the word held a very different connotation to me: it signaled great heaviness and panic.

Since the word "abandon" has such contrasting meanings, my brain fumbles when I hear it. The definitions are braided in my mind, so I have to intentionally untangle them. On the one hand, I hear a promise: "He will not leave you or abandon you."

And on the other hand, I hear a possibility. Others may leave us.

The night before facing the cross Jesus took some disciples to the garden for prayer. He needed their support before he had to face such terror alone. Yet they did not heed his request to join him in prayer; instead, they fell asleep. They abandoned him in the hours he needed them most. In such a heavy scene, there is comfort since Jesus knows what it feels like when we experience those scary waves of abandonment.

The unbraiding then is this—promise versus possibility. God will never leave us, but people may. I just need to be clear about who I hold on to and to whom I extend grace.

God calls Himself "Immanuel"—God with us. Such a

counter to feeling alone. I think that is why I love this name of God so much. I shrink at the thought of being abandoned again or having my son feel abandoned, but that is only part of the story. Immanuel reminds us we are never alone.

He doesn't say, "You need to go." He says, "I will never let you go." There lies all the difference.

Chapter 23

Armor of God

The Rule of Saint Benedict says, "Always we begin again." I learned about this phrase through Leanna Tankersley's book *Begin Again*. It has been a lifeline with Lukas when our day jolts down the wrong path. I whisper to him "Always we begin again." And then we let all that is hindering our relationship fade away, and we start anew.

This phrase became a touchstone as we launched into more toilet training. Leanna writes:

"We love the idea of doing things once and for all, but this is not where meaning is found. We don't take communion once and for all. We don't love our spouse once and for all. We don't parent once and for all...We return—in what becomes a sacred connection—to the mundane task, to the moment. And then we do it again. Over and over. Again...This is the task of humanity. To return. To reinvest. To breathe. To begin again. The focus is on the process, the participation, not the product. Ever."

Yes, I would love to do toilet training once and for all, but I sensed I would be saying, "we begin again" quite a bit in the days to come.

When we started our most recent "Take Four" (Lukas now almost nine), I walked into this training with a growing dread. I sensed the battlefield ahead. I recognize how vastly different a soldier's experience is from mine, such that I greatly hesitate to even note it, yet there were some comparisons worth exploring. We were both fighting for independence: they sought our country's freedom while I sought Lukas'. We both had battlegrounds where the fight for control took place: their battleground probably felt far too vast while my battleground felt far too small. And as I battled my son's desire for control, I saddened to think I was somehow viewing him as my enemy to beat.

Yet our end goals were quite different. The soldier's goal was to have his opponent surrender, while I sensed that God was trying to teach *me* to surrender, to give up what I couldn't control.

Lukas wasn't the only one in training. God had me in training through this process, too. I didn't really like the arena where He was trying to teach me, this confining bathroom; nevertheless, it was where important lessons awaited me.

After telling a friend about my struggle to stop connecting toilet training with a battleground, she reminded me of the armor God beckons us to wear. "Maybe there is something for you to explore in this battle image before you dismiss it," she suggested. So I turned to Paul's New Testament letter where the armor of God is found. What caught my attention the most was the "belt of truth." We are to fasten around our waist, our very core, God's words. Since lies were speaking the loudest on this current battleground, I knew my starting point was to identify the lies: You should be embarrassed; everyone else toilet trained their children on their own. You aren't enough for the task. You are letting your son down. Yes, lies I had heard before.

Now what were the truths I needed to fasten around my center instead so I could stop falling prey to these lies? God seemed to say: "You can't do this alone; I never intended my children to live life that way." "You are enough. Just as you are. I called all of my children 'very good' before you did anything." "You are fighting for your son, a worthy cause. I know how hard it is to see your son mistreated...I experienced that, too."

He says He will never leave us. Not even in a mundane bathroom. He can make all spaces sacred. There were many mundane places in my life where I still needed to invite God's presence...it was just, for now, I was learning how to invite Him into the bathroom. I guess there are different rooms in my life that feel more comfortable than others to invite God into, but He wants access to them all, so I was working on opening up the doors that I would much rather keep shut.

Just as Lukas hasn't relinquished control very easily, I also have been slow to relinquish control. Like me, God must feel like this battle takes place in a cramped, messy room...otherwise known as my heart. But He doesn't give up on me no matter how many "takes" it takes.

And so I grab Lukas' hand and we slowly walk back into the bathroom.

Chapter 24

Losing Control

"The first-grade class is going on a field trip to see a production of *Curious George*. Would you be able to join us?" Lukas' teacher asked. I love any opportunity to see theater and so I quickly jumped at being a chaperone. But as the day drew nearer, anxious thoughts began to emerge. I bristled at the thought of being watched. The other parents would certainly look on and the teachers would observe what I did when Lukas hit those bumpy moments. I looked forward to George's curiosity, but I did not look forward to my fellow adults' curiosity. They might be eager to see how I control Lukas, how I get him to behave…and they would soon learn the truth.

I don't.

Try as I might to keep him under control, most of the time I scramble to redirect him, to remember the most recent pointer from his behavior therapist, or to turn the situation into a song. Instead of witnessing how I kept him under control, what they would see was how I sputtered and faltered.

With the field trip merely one day away, I went out for a walk. I began to tell God all about my fears, beseeching Him to help me keep composure, and probably more than anything, asking Him to give Lukas "a good day." If he had a good day, then it would look like I was able to control him. But in the midst of my pleading for control, I heard God whisper: "Show them that you love him."

Hmmm? This day that I longingly entitled "Control," God just renamed "Love."

I could do that.

That was what they really needed to see after all. If his classmates only witnessed my focus on compliance, then they might believe control was the highest goal for Lukas' life. And if he refused my control, he would be left looking like a nuisance, an unruly kid. But if his classmates saw me loving him in the midst of his different ways, then they might learn that the higher goal is to love even when it is difficult, and to draw near to "different." Different doesn't need to be re-shaped into "normal," it often just needs to be loved in its different-ness.

This really settled into my soul as I thought about God. Of course He would tell me that I didn't need to show people I could control my children...*He* doesn't do that. Look at God's children. The Bible is teeming with stories of how His children walked their own way and weren't in His control. My task was simply to show them how to love Lukas in the midst of any potential struggle since that is what God does. He loves us even when we are out of control, unruly, and far from His higher hopes.

So when Lukas started to flap his arms in excitement during the performance, I didn't try to reign his arms in; I just glanced his way and delighted in his joy. And when he dropped to the ground rather than following his classmates back to the bus, I grabbed him in my arms and gave him an extra squeeze.

He wasn't controlled that day. His behavior was far from perfect. But he was loved.

That is the kind of day we all seek to have.

The imperfections aren't swept away, they are certainly seen, but the arms that greet those imperfections don't wrangle them to the ground or try to eclipse them. They simply wrap themselves around the loved one. Just like God does.

Chapter 25

Power of a Name

It was 2nd period. After teaching my first English class, I sat down to catch my breath from the morning scramble and organize the rest of my day. I breathed in the silence of the empty classroom.

The quiet was short lived as a panting student screamed, "Miss Berg, come quick. A fight just broke out at the top of the stairs."

My first thought was *and you rushed to get me of all people?* I am not even 5'4", I failed the flex arm hang in PE class, and I am wearing heels! I thought of a handful of other teachers more suited to stop a fight. But I ran down the hallway without a clue of how I might help.

A crowd gathered around as two boys pushed and punched each other, frighteningly close to the stairwell where even more damage could occur. One of the boys was a student from my first period class; I put my hand on his shoulder and said, "Ian, come with me."

And most surprising…he did.

I didn't sound authoritative or demanding in that moment; if anything, my voice slightly quivered. And yet Ian followed anyway. I wasn't sure why this worked, but I was relieved both boys were safe.

Many years later I received a call about my own son, a 2nd grader, who was being disruptive at school. I needed to pick him up since he was kicking classmates and wiping his nose on them (lovely!).

When I arrived at the school, he squirmed around on the floor and refused to get up. I tried my same "Ian trick" by simply touching Lukas' shoulder and saying his name, but Lukas didn't respond. So, I scooped him up under his shoulders and trudged him back to the car.

Once I secured him in the car seat, after quite a physical battle, I could feel my anger rising. I was mad at the school for sending him home—wouldn't that just make Lukas equate bad behavior with a free pass to leave? I was mad at Lukas for being so aggressive with me and so hard-hearted with his aide—he refused to apologize before we left. And I was mad at myself for battling his stubbornness with my own stubbornness—I certainly wasn't modeling better behavior for him.

Feeling at a loss, I started to sing Margaret Becker's song "Say the Name." I hadn't thought of that song since my college days, but it was the song that came to mind: "Say the Name, Jesus / say the Name that soothes the soul / the Name of gentle healing / and peace immutable."

In Lukas' gravelly voice, he said, "Stop singing." But I told him I would not. I would sing over him. After more singing, I put my forehead against Lukas' and started to pray. I sensed Lukas' light was being stomped on. It was becoming so dim I could barely see it. It was being puffed out like the song "This Little Light of Mine," and I had to hover over Lukas' embers and ask God to breathe life back into him.

My prayers were strained; I couldn't muster the words I needed. I fumbled in fighting this battle and like my student, Ian, I just wanted someone to call me out of it, so I didn't have to fight.

I went back to singing, my attempt to *begin again*, and I soon realized that it wasn't just Lukas that needed Jesus' name sung over him. I, too, needed this name: "I'll say the name that has heard my cry / has seen my tears and wiped them dry / from now until the end of time / I'll say the Name." Lukas softened. His forehead stopped pressing against mine like a competing bull and soon my cheek was resting next to his. We had been called out of the fight. God was, yet again, reminding me we don't journey alone.

Later I recalled the conversation I had with our school's dean the day Ian was in his fight. The dean explained to me that when a brawl breaks out usually people want a reason to save face and end the fight. Ian just needed to hear his name; it gave him permission to get out. Lukas and I needed to hear a name that day, too. The name Margaret Becker's song placed upon my lips.

Chapter 26

Start with our Toes

After the momentous week of meeting Sarah and her birth mom, I was eager to introduce Sarah to everyone. Since we had just moved to Florida, and most of our family was still in Chicagoland, these introductions would have to be postponed; however, my Mom and Lukas were going to pick us up from the airport so Lukas could be the first to meet his new sister.

The plane ride had been rather tense. A few rows ahead of us a baby screamed while two different passengers reacted harshly. "Enough!" one man gruffly barked. Then a woman chimed in, "Stop it!" These disgruntled passengers stirred a flight attendant to come to the family's aid. Even though the seat belt light was still on, she gave the father permission to walk the aisle and tame his son's bellowing cries. I knew I was not in the midst of a compassionate crowd, so I tirelessly bounced Sarah in my arms the rest of the flight. I did not want us to be the next ones under attack. When we landed and I could finally relax, I was ready for the respite of falling into my own mother's arms.

As we came up the ramp, I was quick to spot my Mom and Lukas. Lukas was donning a bright yellow and blue shirt that boasted "Big Brother." And there was my mom brimming with the desire to cradle Sarah, ready to let her tears of joy peak out. Yet as I approached them, Lukas shook his head "no" while his lower lip slowly puckered. Ah, this image quickly tore at my heart. I wanted Lukas to love his new sibling, but I could see fear creeping into his eyes. He kept evading my arms that wanted to bundle him close.

As we all settled into the car, I relished seeing that Lukas would no longer be in the backseat by himself. He had a new playmate to share life's experiences with. However, this glow did not last for long as Sarah soon began to wail. Since Lukas is very sensitive to loud, explosive noises, he was tortured by the piercing sounds of her screams. Immediately he began to wail himself, digging the heels of his hands into his ears to block out the racket. I quickly maneuvered myself into the backseat, only able to fit one butt cheek in between the car seats. I was contorted, uncomfortable, and unable to console either child. We were only about halfway home when I said a sharp, "Stop it!" to Sarah. It didn't take long for me to turn into that woman from the plane, the one whose behavior made me grimace.

My mom calmly asked me, "Did you just scold, Sarah? Sweetie, she is a baby." Yet there I was agitated that Sarah would disrupt Lukas so much upon our first time together. It didn't take long before I, too, was crying in the backseat. This was NOT how I imagined our homecoming! Since Lukas' birth arrival was fraught with anxiety, I yearned to experience a different kind of arrival with Sarah. However, my vision of joyously embracing was being usurped by our discomfort in one another's proximity. Smushed together in that backseat amidst piercing wails, we were not having a celebratory union.

We eventually escaped the car that night, but other long

car rides continued to be a challenge. When Sarah would cry in the car, it sent shock waves through Lukas' system, a sensory overload for sure. I tried everything I could fathom: I played classical music in hopes of soothing them, I opened all of the windows to try to diffuse the audible pressure, I counted to thirty really slowly (many, many times), and I even made-up songs to try and entertain the kids. I remember my Dad would tell me and my brother Hansel and Gretel bedtime stories using Kimmsel and Brettel instead. We were delighted to have our names as part of the story. When I tried this very same tactic with my children, they seemed to cry all the more. Nothing worked.

The chaos in the car was unsettling, but I think there was a deeper discomfort in me. It was a question that lurked in the back of my mind: How would Lukas learn to love this little girl if she signaled to him pain and deep discomfort? I loved growing up with siblings. My brothers are in the snapshots of my favorite childhood memories and I wanted this for Lukas, too. We knew he would have the steadfast love of his older siblings, Steven, Holly and Kurtis, but they were all off on their own journeys, so Sarah was the one Lukas would grow up with. I wanted him to love the gift of a sister, but this relationship was off to a very rocky start.

I knew I had to do something. I had to change the connection he had with her. When he looked at her, he just saw the potential of a squalling baby. So what did I do? I started with their toes. I simply allowed their toes to touch, to connect them in the smallest of ways. When Lukas was first born and had to stay in the hospital for an extended time, Eric and I slept many nights on a friend's couch. We couldn't lie next to each other, so we put our heads at opposite ends and simply let our toes touch. This small act gave me tremendous comfort at that time, so I thought it might be a good place for Lukas and Sarah to start.

Then we slowly worked up from there: he would touch her knees, her tummy, her hand, her head. Such small steps allowed him to become comfortable with her. He relished her laugh when he tickled her; he now associated her with something more than just her cries. He drew closer to her and started to notice her funny faces, her bright eyes, her reaching for him.

Now when bedtime arrives, she will bend over from my arms to give Lukas a goodnight kiss. Few people know how sacred that moment is to me. To witness their joy of connecting has profound beauty in light of how they use to cause each other to recoil. We went from him backing away, lips curled under, to him leaning in. We went from toes touching to lips touching. We went from dismissal to belonging.

I think this may be a more pronounced version of what we all go through. The fear that moves our feet away from others when they may seem threatening or unknown. The discomfort that comes when someone is saying something that is too grating for our ears to hear. The narrow label we can attach to someone when we have only given ourselves a limited space to know her.

But what awaits us after we move beyond the fear, discomfort, and labeling is the slow emergence of connection.

Somehow when we interact with people who are out of our comfort zone, we need to discover what it looks like to start with our toes.

Chapter 27

Kind to Our Core

One of Blanche DuBois' most memorable lines in *A Streetcar Named Desire* is "I have always depended on the kindness of strangers." She kept afloat by unknown people caring for her. I found this line to be a quaint phrase when I was first introduced to Blanche in college. Even more than that, I found it to be a pitiable motto to live by. If only she had better connections with her family and friends, she wouldn't need strangers so much. I was sad that she seemed tossed about with nowhere else to turn except strangers.

Yet her words were about to take on a deeper meaning.

Eric had work commitments that would keep him in Crystal Lake for the week, so I was caring for our children by myself. No matter how hard I tried to fill my tank beyond what was needed, I always found the day before his return extremely draining. On this particular Sunday, I was quite aware I was nearing empty. However, all I had to do was bring the kids to church and to the grocery store...then we would huddle in to read books and watch movies.

When we neared the church's steps, Lukas wiggled out of holding my hand and ran back towards the parking lot. We learned through behavior therapy that chasing Lukas just reinforced this behavior; he found it all to be a fun game. I hated chasing him, particularly with Sarah in my arms, but the fear of a car hitting him had me racing to capture his hand. Then as we neared the steps again, he dropped to the ground. If I set my daughter down, she would scurry off herself, but it was near impossible for me to pick him up while holding on to her. A man at the top of the stairs said, "Can I grab a bag or a baby for you?"

And without my usual hesitation, I said, "Yes, please," handing him Sarah. I was finally able to hoist Lukas up each stair, as he continued to fight and frustrate me. This gentle faced man must have seen my exasperation, so he offered to carry Sarah all the way to the childcare doors.

When we were saying our goodbyes, I could only muster a meager, "Thanks." I think I may have whispered it even. Although there was so much more I wanted to say, I could feel my throat clench. His kindness wasn't a gesture that made me want to smile. It was much bigger than that. It was a kindness that made me want to weep.

I imagine he walked away thinking he did a small thing that morning. And yet to me, he gave me dignity in a moment that I could feel myself deflated. When I wanted to crumple right next to Lukas at the foot of the stairs, he not only picked up Sarah, but he picked up me. That felt like a very big thing.

When I couldn't get Lukas to follow me up the stairs at church, I felt the bitter sting of failure. Church seems to be the epitome of where we want our children to be on their best behavior, but we were both falling short. After a week of struggle, I was turning to church to be a respite, a place where I could get sewn back together. And there was this stranger that blessed me with kindness. Blanche's words were beginning to resonate more deeply.

In those moments of feeling overwhelmed that week, my frustration and desire to lash out charged their way forward. It had been a long time since I had experienced anger. Growing up, my father had occasional outbursts. They made me quick to cower and avert my eyes; I didn't like how anger could so easily contort a face. I watched how my Mom tiptoed around my Dad and found ways to soothe him back to neutral. Somewhere in my college years, I vowed I would never marry someone with a temper. I did not want to live in a household vulnerable to anger. And so I married a man who has a very gentle demeanor. Eric's voice is like a radio set at a lower volume.

Nevertheless, that week revealed to me something that punctured my soul: I had become the person I was trying to keep out of our house. I was the one yelling with my teeth clenched, slapping Lukas' hand when he plunged it into the toilet yet again, and howling at no one in particular. I may have kept a man out of our house who could explode in anger, but me and my anger resided in that home, and I was the one frightening my sweet children.

So yes, my kids needed kindness that Sunday morning. I needed kindness that morning. And I needed the courage to take the next breath and *begin again*.

I have always loved kind people; I think we all do. I love being in their midst. I marvel at how they actively show people they love them. I treasure how they can make someone light up by an encouraging word or action. To me, it seemed like they were good at taking the focus off of themselves in order to put it on others. However, I was discovering that they needed to practice kindness to themselves before they could embody kindness to others.

Jesus said, "Love your neighbor as yourself." Sadly, we often lop off those last two words. However, Jesus is saying our love for others springs from how we love ourselves. I had only witnessed people loving their neighbors. That was the kindness I knew. I wasn't privy to those quiet and private moments when people experienced God's love and learned how to love themselves. Those times when they breathed in His grace and goodness, so they could breathe out any anger or frustration. Those moments when they learned how to speak to themselves with kindness as a balm to any scorn or judgment. How are we kind to ourselves? I was starting to learn: We treat ourselves as we want to treat others.

As the songwriter, Paul Williams, says, "You know every act of kindness is a little bit of love we leave behind." That man at church Sunday morning was God's hands to me. He carried what I could not carry in that moment. His kindness, his "little bit of love," did not feel like a small thing. He was manna for my day.

Chapter 28

Weighty Matters

From a young age, I always dreaded Monday mornings. Not for the same reasons that others may dread Mondays—another week of school or work. I dreaded Mondays because they signaled another three day fast. In my weekly panic, I aimed to lose the three-four pounds I cyclically gained all before Wednesday night's weigh-in. These weigh-ins took place at our dance studio and introduced us to the professional practice we might encounter if we pursued a career in dance. So Monday mornings ushered in my silent goodbyes to substantial food.

Breakfast was easy enough to skip; I just slept in later so I didn't have time to miss it. Then for lunch I bought a lemon ice, something I could slowly suck on while others ate their sack lunches brimming with sandwiches, chips, and Hostess goodies. I never wanted anyone to notice my meagre lunch because after all my goal was for others to think I was naturally skinny. If they knew I worked hard at maintaining my weight, it somehow lost its luster. I wanted skinny to be *who I was*, my natural self, not something I labored to attain. I pretended I had a small appetite, making me feel dainty, while my stomach groaned and gripped at me, reminding me what a liar I was.

If my panic was especially high from overindulging

that past weekend, I took a diet pill to curb my appetite. Not only was I trying to fool others that I was rarely hungry, I was also trying to fool myself. Even bedtime wasn't free from the stranglehold of my weight. I would open the window to the cold night air and climb into bed donning plastic pants designed to make me sweat. It was my last-ditch effort to increase my metabolism and hopefully lose one more pound before daybreak. There was no rest in this weight loss process.

Then Wednesday would roll around, a day of unsettling nerves. I feared each step that moved me closer to Ms. Nancy's look of condemnation. Wearing pink tights that showed my dimpled thighs, and a burgundy leotard that put dents in my hips because of my added fat there, I may as well have been naked...I felt incredibly exposed. She didn't need the scale to tell me I didn't have a dancer's body. The classroom wall was full of mirrors I faced each day, and this was proof enough that my body didn't measure up to her expectations. Yet each week I had to slink into this back room, feeling strangely small while simultaneously feeling far too big. I had snuck into the back room many times before to practice my weigh-in, and if I stood with my feet closer to the numbers I could carve off about a pound of weight. More deception. Everything about this scale brought out the liar in me.

And so there I would stand with my full breasts and wide hips, with no real waist in between, as the pointer rattled back and forth before settling on a number. I held my breath as my chest stiffened. *"Please, please, please be under 110."* Then I won't get a lecture or her steely stare of disappointment. Please don't make my self-worth be all about a number that I can scarcely attain. Please don't make me scramble to do this all over again next week.

Please stop trying to make me a skinny girl when it feels like an impossible task.

I dreaded Ms. Nancy's words I had heard before: "You are getting fat," "You can't dance at this weight," "I may have to change the casting since you won't fit in that costume." Or, her most memorable: "What does it feel like to be pleasantly plump?" Those words she didn't say in the privacy of that back room; those words she kept for rehearsal later that night so everyone heard them.

Although people felt bad when she singled me out, they also took a fresh look at how my bra cut into my back fat, or how the extra inches at my waistline peeked over my tights. These weren't the smooth lines of a ballerina. The other girls, who barely needed bras and wore leotards that slinked over their taut figures, fulfilled the image of a ballerina.

To add further embarrassment, Ms. Nancy then directed me to practice a shoulder lift. I was never a good jumper and I was rather scared of this lift. Usually I imagined barreling over my partner's shoulder and landing on my head behind him, but now that I was newly named "pleasantly plump," I assumed such momentum would be impossible. While I tried to defy my new label, my partner's elbows wavered as he heaved me onto his shoulder. Ms. Nancy was right...I was plump, but there was nothing pleasant about it.

During my senior year of high school, I vowed to never step on a scale again. I couldn't be a number any longer. My clothes would be my new scale, and they would tell me how I was doing. It just started feeling too heavy to routinely disappoint myself.

Gladly, I found new freedom away from the scale and

the word "diet." I was no longer succumbing to that body image monster, and so he shrank. Yet there were remnants that I noticed. I often shuddered at a touch from a man since it drew attention to my pudgy waist or rippled thigh. I still dreaded summer parties that called for bathing suits. And I sheepishly explained to nurses, health teachers, and fitness centers why I needed to step on the scale backwards: "I do not want to know my weight." I knew all too well the whirl of emotions that number could unleash in me.

But this monster simply slept under the surface only to rear its nasty head during a vulnerable time: the sacred season of carrying Lukas. Not only did Ms. Nancy rob me of enjoying my childhood figure, the innocence of a young body developing and embracing its new curves, but more devastatingly, she robbed me of delighting in my with-child figure.

I couldn't grasp seeing a pregnant body as beautiful; I only saw it as being far from thin. I felt out of control with my eating habits. My nauseous stomach was quieted by potato chips and vanilla milkshakes, items I had never previously indulged. When I meekly asked Dr. Moses, "How am I doing with my weight?" tears quickly welled in my eyes and that old stiffness in my chest returned. How could I be so shallow to ask this? I could pretend that I was asking on my son's behalf, as if his health was my concern, but that would just be another lie. I knew I was yet again in the grip of my old wounds. The scale loomed larger than it had a right to. I was supposed to be pleasantly plump now, but those words had already been ruined for me.

My struggle with body image comes into sharp focus as I raise my children. I look at their bodies and see God's artistry. I join God and say, "Very good." The unique way they were created is VERY good. I celebrate both what is deemed beautiful by our culture and what remains outside that definition. Lukas' green, smiling eyes and long, lean frame as well as his underbite and flat-footed walk; Sarah's long eyelashes and luscious, curly hair as well as her pudgy stomach and gummy smile. I think we understand this lesson with our children more than we do with ourselves. We treasure every morsel of their being, counting it ALL beauty, while we can't gift ourselves that same acceptance and loving gaze.

I have spent the majority of my life being unkind to my body—taking what others might have said and saying far worse. Looking at her far more critically than anyone else has done. I have been her worst bully. After all she has done for me, she must feel hurt, shunned, unrecognized, and underappreciated.

I shudder to think how I can possibly teach Lukas to love all of who he is when I struggle to do it myself. Just as the world told me my body didn't fit the mold, he is going to hear those same insidious whispers about his body. But my battle cry for him is *You are beautiful as you are.*

My padded hips and his flattened nose...beautiful.
My wide waist and his wide smile...beautiful.

The first Christmas Eric and I celebrated as a couple he painted an abstract portrait of me. Viewers wouldn't know it is me, but he pointed out a feature that captured something he loved: my crooked smile. I returned to old photos to look for this. Yes, the left side of my smile dropped lower than my right. So when I thought of it, I tried to not smile so earnestly when we took pictures. That extra energy seemed to push part of my lip downward. Funny how something I tried to correct in photos was the very thing he celebrated.

Somehow, I think that is how God is. He looks at those nuances in who we are, even the ones we try to hide or desperately change, and He celebrates them. It is what I do when I look at my children. It is what we need to do with ourselves as well.

It is why my scale can't be something that I stand on, but rather a loving gaze that I live under. The gaze God gives us. The gaze loved ones give us. And the gaze I was learning to give myself.

Chapter 29

Training for Two Continues

A return trip to Disney World gleamed on the horizon. Since we were in the midst of toilet training "take four," we were quick to remember how our last Disney visit thwarted any progress we had made. We would have to hold firm to our routine. Yet, I wanted Disney to be about the fanciful, the imagination, the magic...not about a toilet schedule.

Breathing in the Magic Kingdom and all it encompassed brought out the best in Lukas. He gladly walked beside us and didn't even mind waiting in lines (since we had the special needs fast pass, the lines we faced were shorter than most). His face beamed on the rollercoaster, even though he did keep his hand over my mouth to ensure I wouldn't scream and ruin it by piercing his sensitive ears. He danced with the bears at the Country Bear Jamboree, marveled at all of the fish during Little Mermaid's "Under the Sea," pointed out hippos on the Jungle Cruise, and delighted in finally getting to drive a car at Tomorrowland. At home, his attempts at sitting in the driver's seat were always quickly snatched away from him. Disney truly was a land of possibilities.

When we returned to our hotel, weary yet basking in

the memories of the day, we quickly put the kids in pjs and snuggled into bed. Yet up popped Lukas with a spring to his step. He went into the bathroom on his own initiative and came out with a glowing smile. After even more self-initiated trips to the bathroom, we were so hopeful that the strides he made in Disney, a place where we had previously lost headway, would lead to greater strides upon our return home.

However, it didn't take long to realize that any progress we made did not return with us. We were back to his dropping and battling our invitations to the bathroom. My hopelessness returned. I was tired of being disappointed. I was tired of rallying and feigning a positive energy. I was tired of toilet training.

But as I was pouring my coffee the next morning, my eyes fixed on a small sign sitting there. I was given this plaque by our pastor's wife and relished how it highlighted my word for the year. For the past three years, instead of making New Year's resolutions, I prayerfully found a word to set that year's intention. The word for this year was "Believe," and there it was staring back at me. I could see God's timing in prompting this word—it was a year I struggled to believe Lukas would ever become toilet trained. As I had previously noticed that "toil" was in the word "toilet," I now noticed that "lie" sat in the middle of the word "believe."

What lies were trying to strangle away my belief? The lie "this will never happen" needed to be replaced with faith—believing in what we cannot see. The lie "I am not steadfast enough to endure this challenge" needed to be replaced with "God is steadfast and sees us through it all." I was back to fighting against lies and trying to fasten on a belt of truth instead.

Since I lately think the lies are winning, all of this time in a bathroom feels like a waste. I don't know that the scheduled toilet times or the overcorrecting will work, so I become weary and often want to give up. Then God reminded me of Joshua and the Battle of Jericho from the Hebrew scriptures. God told Joshua and his men to walk around the walls of Jericho each day for six days. Then on the seventh day, they were to walk around the walls seven times in order to win this battle. I often wonder what would have happened if they stopped after their sixth go around? I wouldn't blame them. They had to be tired and not fully convinced they heard God's directive correctly. But if they hadn't persevered and followed even when it felt foolish, they wouldn't have witnessed the miracle.

I don't want to be the one that gives up during one of those final laps. Like Joshua, I want to witness what it looks and feels like to make it through that seventh lap when the walls fall down. Walls won't win here either, so Lukas and I tread on.

Chapter 30

Stable Sitting

Something was pricking at my heart. I called my Mom and asked, "Why does our happiness have to be linked to our children's happiness? It feels way too codependent." My days seem to be stamped by the words Lukas' aide says at pick-up: "He had a terrific day." Ah, now my day is wonderful! Or... "Unfortunately, he had a very challenging day." Alas, now my day has taken a turn for the worse.

My mom said, "There is an adage that says we are only as happy as our least happy child."

I simply replied, "I don't like it. I should be able to have a great day even when Lukas is having a terrible one."

But it doesn't seem to work like that. And when you have a child that has a fair number of challenging days, this interconnectedness can feel heavy.

We were just finishing a very positive evening at horse therapy. Lukas giggled as his horse, Clyde, trotted. Lukas' smile beamed and he repeatedly gave me the thumbs up sign (I think he was supposed to be holding on to the reins!).

Then when they were done, he started to walk towards me, but impulsively changed course and ran back to the barn. I knew all behavior was communication, so I suspected he was telling me he wanted more time with the horses; he didn't want this evening to end. But as I tried to put language to what I thought he was feeling, he drew farther away from me. Ultimately, he fell limp to the ground and started squealing. Whatever he was trying to tell me had anguished notes to it...that was the most I could decipher. My clawing to get hold of him was countered by his writhing. We fumbled and fought each other. He added more squealing and I joined in with low growls. We were losing all dignity. I couldn't move him or coax him to the car, and my attempts made the situation far worse. I had to simply sit with him in the dust.

My insides started their own kind of squealing. This was terribly uncomfortable; I wanted to hurry the pain away or run from it. I imagined one of those magnetic drawing boards where you can swiftly erase the chaotic scribblings of a child. One swipe brought you back to a clean slate. That is what I wanted to do. I longed to retreat behind the locked doors of our car where I wouldn't have to pretend such a scene didn't bother me. Deeply bother me.

If I saw this scene on a video, it would look like Lukas and I were in a brawl. Me fighting to get him back on his feet and him fighting to keep his body prone on the ground. I hated seeing us this way.

He had such ache, such anger. And all I could do was remain in the dirt and bear witness to his pain. I couldn't fix it or take it away. I could just remain. My thoughts circled back to the image of my Grandma sitting beside her son.

Why did my inability to help Lukas gnaw at me so? Jesus doesn't take away our pain. He comes and sits in it with us. He is not afraid to wrestle with any of his sons...just ask Jacob. He is not afraid to be without dignity...just look at the scene when he was knocked around by the Romans and mocked with a crown of thorns.

As I tried to sit with Lukas in his pain, Jesus came and sat beside me in mine.

Maybe motherhood isn't just a picture of us serenely walking beside our children. Maybe it is also a picture of us struggling with them and then sitting beside them in the dirt. I am slowly learning that I need to stay in the difficult circumstances long enough for them to work on my soul. Although the moments can feel excruciating at times, the lessons I learn there are swollen with wisdom.

As I reflected on this day, and so many others like it, two questions arose. I felt Lukas silently asking me:

Will you love me here?

> *In this muck. In this scuffle. In this anguish.*

And will you remain?

> *When dignity seems fleeting…*
> *When great discomfort sets in…*
> *When turning away feels very tempting*

I think those are the same questions I silently ask Jesus.

The scene in the stable wasn't pretty. On days like those, I wish we didn't have to be so interconnected. I wish I could fly to the tune of my own happiness and not feel the tug of what lies inside Lukas' heart. Maybe the words of Frederick Buechner from *Now & Then* need to settle deeper into my heart:

> "If by some magic you could eliminate the pain you are caused by the pain of someone you love, I for one cannot imagine working such magic because the pain is so much a part of the love that

the love would be vastly diminished, unrecognizable, without it. To suffer in love for another's suffering is to live life not only at its fullest but at its holiest."

All I know is the dirt that was all over us at day's end is not the end of our story. Ezekiel knows firsthand how God's stories end. In a prophetic vision, Ezekiel looked over a valley full of dry human bones. It was a scene of desolation. But God's stories don't end in ashes or death, or in our case, dirt from a horse's stable. His stories end with Him breathing life back into those bones or any of our dry, barren places.

And so we wait upon His breath.

Part IV

Let Him Shine
new insights,
emerging light, hope renewed

"The wound is the place where the light enters you."
— Rumi

"If you are trying to transform a brutalized society
into one where people can live in dignity and hope,
you begin with the empowering of the most
powerless. You build from the ground up."
— Adrienne Rich

Chapter 31

It is Quite Simple, Really

I have noticed something.

It is quite simple, really.

When Lukas was a toddler and I was away for a weekend or so, I was greeted by all of the features that revealed his diagnosis: a broad smile, upturned eyes, and a flat bridge above his nose. I didn't see these on a daily basis. Only when I greeted him from afar.

On most days, I was busy playing airplane with him, cradling him in my lap for story time, or racing him around the island in our kitchen.

Or maybe it was even more mundane than that...I was teaching him how to spoon his own yogurt, buckling him into his car seat, or singing any song that allowed me to brush his teeth.

My days weren't spent with those establishing shots so often used in films, but with close-ups. With daily activities that kept our faces near one another.

And so I have learned a simple principle of life from Lukas: when we love each other up close, our frailties fade away. Yes, we may see the sleepers in each other's eyes or become more aware of a crooked smile, but somehow, we find these qualities prized peculiarities. From a distance, they are imperfections; up close, they are endearments.

I believe Lukas has been silently teaching me how to love others better. If he were to put it simply, I believe he would merely say, "Move closer."

From afar, it is too easy to judge or to scrutinize our differences. Too easy to allow fear to take hold and keep us at a distance. Why can't that large birthmark or burn mark become a favorite painting on a friend's face? Why can't those crossed eyes remind us to look into that soul and not just stop at the pupils? Why can't that flat bridge be a unique place to land a daily kiss?

Move closer. It is quite simple, really.

Chapter 32

Living in Your Lane

Lukas says, "I love- ah you" a bit like his Italian Papa Joe might say it. Although I consider re-teaching him how to say this phrase, I wonder why I would want it any different? This is his heart's unique way of expressing itself. My desire to alter the way he says it comes from wanting him to be like everyone else. I suspect we want our kids to fit in long before they have that desire. Then once they do want to be like others, we tirelessly persuade them against such conformity!

We seem to spend the first part of our lives trying to normalize ourselves in order to fit in; then we spend the rest of our lives trying to figure out how we are unique and set apart.

I guess Lukas magnifies the hard-earned beauty of living in one's own lane sooner than most children would. I don't even think he wants to live in the more populated lanes. His pace is his own and his ways of doing things are his own. Consequently, I am constantly having to unravel my desires for him from his desires for himself. It takes more intentional listening to what *isn't* being said; it takes more noticing of when I eclipse his life with *my* hopes for his life.

I remember the summer I longed to become a swimmer.

I studied the experts and tried to copy their freestyle strokes, breathing patterns, and launches off the pool's edge. But ultimately, I discovered I was more comfortable doing the side stroke. I couldn't go as fast as the others, but I found more ease in this form. I suspect Lukas can relate.

I have noticed that when I find someone else's lane appealing, I feel lured to join her lane. The person often emanates joy, a settled quality, and a sense that her best gifts are fully manifested in this lane. It is magnetic. But if I allow myself to adopt someone else's lane rather than carving out my own, I lose the beautiful discovery of how God has given me a different story and so a different lane. Living in our own lane is both honoring the gifts we have been given and choosing to renounce envy.

In Parker Palmer's book *Let Your Life Speak* he says:

> "If we are to live our lives fully and well, we must learn to embrace the opposites, to live in a creative tension between our limits and our potentials. We must honor our limitations in ways that do not distort our nature, and we must trust and use our gifts in ways that fulfill the potentials God gave us."

These guide rails help me serve both Lukas' life and my own.

I think this idea of living in our own lane God puts another way. He tells us we are all one body, but each a different body part: some are eyes, some are hands, some are ears, some are feet. Paul writes in a letter to the Corinthians, "If the whole body were an eye, how would you hear? ... our bodies have many parts, and God has put each part just where he wants it." God doesn't want all of us to be eyes, or in one lane; He wants us to discover which part we are so we can use our gifts for the good of everyone.

What could be perceived as unfortunate—Lukas living in a lane far different from his peers—I now see as a gift. He feels free to be in his own lane much sooner than most. And this beckons me to do the same.

Chapter 33

Reworking Routine into Ritual

I am a 7. For those of you familiar with the enneagram, that means I love variety, I aim to keep options open, and I am prone to being scattered (to name just a few of the traits). So when I heard how important routine was for kids with Down syndrome and Autism spectrum disorder, I felt a tension rising in me. How was I ever going to help Lukas with routine when I was someone who preferred variety? I suspect my aversion to routine was rooted in a belief that it opposed creativity. Why repeat something when I could find a fresh, unique way to do it? It didn't help to learn that the word "routine" had the word "mechanically" in its definition. Routine: a set of unchanging and often mechanically performed activities. *Why would I want to implement something mechanical into my days?*

Lukas needed someone who was organized and thrived on structure...that was not me. I always struggled to file my paperwork as a teacher; I preferred to create pile after pile and my crowded desk showed it. Colleagues teased me about my lesson plans written on post-it notes; however, I wasn't trying to write a plan I could use over and over. I liked how their flimsy nature encouraged me to teach the lesson differently the next year since I was sure to lose them before then. One less thing for me to file!

Being a teacher actually motivated me to avoid structure at home. Since my day was organized around school bells and a prescribed order, when I came home, I tried to live counter to that model. I didn't want the clock to continue to dictate my actions, so I rebelled against any set structure when I could.

However, I had to figure out how to serve Lukas' need for routine in the midst of it being both a weakness and nemesis of mine. My colleagues and I routinely reflected on how to adapt our teaching styles to best serve our students, so I had experience working outside my comfort level when it came to teaching. Now I would need to do the same in my classroom of one. Routine and repetition would be key players since that was how Lukas learned best.

What was my path towards helping Lukas? I only knew it would have to draw on my strengths rather than my weaknesses. Suddenly I realized I could use my love for ritual to help me. I am drawn to traditions -- those things we did every year as a kind of marker. Our seasonal traditions stood out the most: a trip to Marshall Field's in Chicago to see the Christmas windows and eat under the 45-foot-tall Christmas tree, a trip to Santa's Village with our cousins for the fun rides and petting zoo, and a picture by each child's tree we planted on their baptism day. I began to see how these outings were a kind of routine and a routine I cherished. Now I just needed to find rituals in our everyday life that I could cherish (and keep!) as well.

We began with the bath and books routine since at least I didn't have to do that every day. And from there I added the "towel song." I needed something to remind Lukas to not dodge off after a bath. All of that dripping water needed to go somewhere besides the slippery tile floor and the rest of the house. So I would snuggle Lukas in a towel, turn him to face the mirror, and then wrap my arms around him. We would gently begin to sway as I used the melody from the song "I Got Rhythm" to sing: "I love my Lukas, I love my Lukas, I love my Lukas, who could ask for anything more?" Both kids loved this routine so much they rushed to hand me a towel if I ever forgot. This success spurred me to uncover more routines to serve as a skeleton for our days.

I was learning that routine didn't suck life out of the moment, it added life. But there was a mental shift I had to do: I needed to take the connotations I had with the word "routine" (boring, redundant, stagnant) and exchange them for the connotations I had with the word "ritual" (comforting, memory-makers, ceremonious). As a woman who starts every day with a cup of coffee and a book, I was surprised I overlooked how routine could be life-giving.

This process of discovery reminded me there is always a way in. So although our days mirrored one another, I treasured that sameness because we had uniquely crafted it for ourselves. Routine was birthing creativity rather than robbing us of it.

I suppose I imagined routine as something that would leave me on a parched and tedious road, yet Lukas has shown me how living life in his lane leads me to a beautiful cul-de-sac, where the motion of walking in that circle is sweetly comforting.

Chapter 34

Beauty in the Wading

After our long Chicago winters, we craved the moment we could finally jump into our kidney-shaped pool; however, my parents held a steadfast rule that until we could swim the pool's length, we had to stay in the shallow water. I was not a fan. *Just get me to the deep end where the excitement lives.* My childlike heart believed life was about diving in, over and over again, not wading in the shallow waters.

God was ready to teach me otherwise.

In so many of my significant life experiences, God closed the diving board to me. Instead of plunging in, I had to enter through the shallow water and wade around awhile.

I am not a naturally patient person. It is probably why I took diet pills as a teenager; I wanted results fast. It is why I love restaurants that give out beepers so I don't have to hang out in their foyer. Instead, I can go do something, like Christmas shopping, while I technically "wait" for a table. Even while I lingered in the waiting room during Lukas' heart surgery, I knew I had to do more than merely sit there and wait. And so I pulled out some yarn to knit.

Let's face it. It feels painful to wait.

Yet God has been teaching me that waiting isn't wasted time. It is a time of preparation.

It is when all of the ingredients in a meal slowly simmer or bake in order to become more tender and flavorful.

It is when the caterpillar forms a chrysalis so it can later fly with gorgeous wings or when a seed buried in the dark dirt waits until spring to reveal its stunning color.

It is when cells become fingers and a heart and a child. It is when parents-to-be start reading baby books, gathering needed items, and interviewing other parents for helpful advice.

My first season of waiting was when I earnestly prayed God would lead me to a husband; I prayed this for over a decade. Meanwhile, I watched other women get engaged with ease, which felt so frustrating. Yet God knew the special circumstances I would one day face, and so He knew I needed to learn how to surrender my timing to someone else's timing. There was purpose and preparation in this time of waiting. Ultimately, I surrendered my dream of getting married (and what I thought it should look like), only to witness how God would later lead me to Eric and re-awaken my hope for a family.

This was my first introduction to the death and resurrection pattern so familiar to God. A dream dies, God breathes life into it again, and then we stand in awe of what has been renewed.

Lukas has also been teaching me how to wait. Because of his diagnosis, every milestone he faced came after an extended time of waiting, of wading in that shallow end of the pool, always with an eye on the deep end. After hours of trying to teach Lukas how to walk, I placed his favorite apple-flavored breakfast bar on an ottoman and watched him finally support his weight as he wobbled towards me. The diving board of a quick and easy plunge is rarely open to us. While most parents wait a year for their child to walk, Lukas didn't walk until he was over two years old. When the waiting was over, I squealed while drops of gladness fell from my eyes. That joy was magnified precisely because we had waited and worked for those first steps for so long.

I vividly remember the day Lukas crawled, the day he walked, the day he said "Mama", the day he put his face in the pool because they all took so MANY days to get to. I don't remember those days as clearly in Sarah's life. Not because they weren't important, but perhaps because they felt inevitable. But that spirit of inevitability robs us of savoring moments we won't ever get back. And that is all moments in life, really. We don't get any of them back.

Sweetly, Lukas has slowed life down for us so that we see moments with a magnifying glass. They become bigger than they might be otherwise. He orients us to treasuring the smallest of moments that are often filled with the grandest of strides.

There is beauty in the wading; yes, beauty in the waiting.

Waiting can be a precious time of inclining our ears and hearts toward God. A time of expectancy. A time of calling us into contentment *before* any gift is received. God is patient. He, too, has to wait. He waits many years for our prodigal hearts to come home. He knows the pain of hearts that go astray, and He knows the joy of their return. He knows the goodness born out of the ashes and He knows death never gets the final word. When we have to wait, maybe it is because He doesn't want us to miss out on the depth of such rejoicing!

Chapter 35

Call of the One

I guess I could call myself a Bible study gal. So many favorite memories spring from gathering around a table to connect with God and others. I loved Henry Blackaby's *Experiencing God* so much I did that study multiple times. One of my leaders gave each of us a scarf with pockets and told us we were to be "pocket people." Putting our hands in the pockets was a gentle reminder to pray for one another. And since it was winter in Chicago, we were putting our hands in those pockets quite often!

When I was pregnant with Lukas, I led Beth Moore's study of *Esther: It's Tough Being a Woman*. In this study, I will always remember the words: "If _____, then God." Whatever may come our way, she wanted to remind us that we never had to face life's difficulties alone. If we had hopelessness over our job, then God. If our marriage was faltering, then God. If we struggled with any wide array of addiction, then God. Simply put, this sentence was about reminding us to turn to God. Those words carried significant weight when we learned Lukas had Down syndrome. My sentence became: "If your child is born with Down syndrome, then God."

Yet one group stands out the most. It was a study called *Listen to My Life* by Sibyl Towner and Sharon Swing, and it was a compilation of visual maps designed to reveal how our life story illuminates themes found in God's grand story. In this group, we shared an extensive timeline of our lives, highlighting moments that made us soar and moments that etched deep wounds into our souls. This process wove our hearts together with greater intimacy and authenticity than I had ever experienced. These were the women who gathered around me and Lukas after toilet training when our hearts needed mending.

After our move to Southwest Florida, I quickly became restless and eager to find a meaningful community. So, I decided to start my own *Listen to My Life* study. I had tried many other ways to meet people, but nothing was satisfying my soul urge to connect on a deeper level.

After getting the word out about this new group, I had around six people who told me they would attend my "come and see" gathering. I had diligently cleaned, baked some mini egg muffins, cut fresh fruit, and borrowed my mom's coffee pot so I could have ten cups of coffee ready for my potential people.

And here is the thing: only one person showed up.

My time away from my children was so rare in those days that I felt pressure to make any time away really count. I took hot yoga instead of regular yoga so I was ensured to sweat; I didn't just go for a walk on the beach, I listened to a podcast while I walked in order to exercise both physically and spiritually. So here I was ready to make the morning "really count" and I was only welcoming one person.

It felt like mockery. My yellow pad of paper filled with notes and planning embarrassed me in that moment. I sheepishly hid this yellow pad and instead decided to learn about the one woman who came.

As I cleaned up all of the leftover food and poured the pot of coffee down the drain, I remembered the story of Jesus going after the one sheep.

I felt like God was asking my heart: Will you go after the one?

I don't think so – it takes too much energy without enough pay off. I would rather stay with the 99 while someone else goes after the one.

But the whisper came again: Will you go after the one?

I don't want to. I want to make sure my time really counts.

The question lingered and pressed in for a different answer: Will you go after the one?

Is that what you are asking me this morning, God? God's question started to sink deeper. I pondered my response: *if my heart is pure in its intent to serve You above all else, then whether you give me 1 or 101 shouldn't matter.*

This all reminded me of hearing a message years ago from Andy Stanley, a visiting pastor speaking at Chicagoland's Willow Creek Community Church. His sermon had a clear point: "Do for one what you wish you could do for everyone." He wanted us to recognize how we often stop ourselves from helping people or organizations in need when the many feels overwhelming. What can our small contribution really add? And so we talk ourselves out of helping at all. But he urged us to see our love for the one as our love for the many. I was being challenged to answer: Does one matter?

Then I thought of how I want my one, my Lukas, to matter enough that others go after his heart. To matter enough that they leave the accolades of the 99 in order to seek this little sheep in need. Like Ms. Lorraine and Ms. Robin do every Sunday. It may feel like a small gesture to the person who is merely with the one, but to the parent of that one, the gesture feels magnanimous. I know.

It goes back to what I learned in Jock Hall and the message etched on Eric's ring: we all want to be chosen.

In the book of Acts there is a story of God beseeching someone to go after one of His sons. God's spirit directed Philip to get up and go to a chariot where an Ethiopian court official was reading the prophet Isaiah. I love how it says that Philip "ran to him." Hardly the sluggish response I had to the one God provided me that morning. Philip's running feet revealed a heart that celebrated meeting who God had for him that day. And this meeting turned into the Ethiopian eunuch getting baptized. The passage ends by saying the eunuch "went on his way rejoicing."

I don't think the eunuch was the only one rejoicing that day. Philip must have rejoiced at being chosen by God to meet such a man, to have the honor of being a part of his journey. And God rejoiced. His Ethiopian son was seen and heard, and this "chance encounter" left him knowing His Father better.

What I deemed as a failed start to my *Listen to My Life* group, God saw as a milestone. It was a chance for me to learn a lesson very dear to His heart: Each *one* matters. He sent Jesus after the one sheep and He sends us after the one sheep. We have all been that one He has gone after at some point in our journey. Now we get to receive that same nudge Philip received as we look for the ones in our midst.

And so I had the perfect number of guests that morning.

Chapter 36

Dread into Dancing

Oh, how I remember the excitement of being invited to a birthday party! Particularly in those elementary years. I was elated to receive an invitation smattered with balloons, promising an afternoon of carefree frolic: pin the tail on the donkey, crazy noisemakers, and a scrumptious ice cream cake. But as of late, that is not my reaction to birthday invitations at all. Lately, my reaction has been dread. Serious dread. And I am not even the one being invited. The invitations are for Lukas.

The first invite was for Sky Zone, a trampoline place. I could already taste the envy that would seep in as I watched other moms gathering to catch up and sip their midday coffees; meanwhile, I would have to be the mid-life body awkwardly jumping around amidst other 1st graders. I knew Lukas would not be able to experience the trampolines on his own, he would need help, so I would have to join him and his classmates in the fray.

On my way to the trampoline area, I passed two moms and said, "Feel sorry for me!" Normally I would keep this sentiment to myself, but I knew I had to name the embarrassment I was feeling. I was the adult wearing the bright, sticky bottom socks, which were not about to let me subtly sneak in. I was the adult crashing the elementary party.

There I was in my yoga pants urging Lukas to jump, to please have fun and make this humiliation worth it! Yet there he was sitting down. Out of fear? Out of stubbornness? Out of let's make Mom really have to work at it?! The only glimmers of delight came when I jumped and he sat nearby. He liked how it made him bounce around on his behind.

Bit by bit, I was able to get him to his knees to bounce and then eventually to his feet. Before too long, there he was jumping with me and smiling with such joy! The embarrassment quickly faded as my attention was no longer on what I looked like, but on celebrating what he looked like. Soon I had two young girls teaching me new moves. I was twirling and attempting split jumps and joining Lukas in his joy.

At the beginning of this party, I thought I was the mom everyone would feel sorry for; but by the end, I felt like the mom everyone would have gladly traded places with. God has a way of surprising us even in the midst of our dreaded moments. I was able to join my son as he found his feet. I didn't have to be set apart or distracted by conversation. I had the privilege of being right beside him, right in the moment. No dread, only dancing.

I wish I could say that this lesson stuck. However, merely three months later I was again reading a birthday invitation and filling with dread. This time Lukas was invited on a party bus that would drive around the community for two hours. The hostess knew she would have a lot of responsibility with thirty kids attending, so she asked if I would join them to keep an eye on Lukas. In order for Lukas to attend, I knew I would have to go. But I am a woman who easily gets car sick, so riding around in a bus for two hours sounded like a recipe for nausea.

As a matter of fact, on one of my first field trips to Chicago with a bus full of high school students, I found myself scurrying off the bus to vomit. Luckily, I had my mom as a fellow chaperone to distract my students while I quickly hovered in a bathroom stall. Now I would not have that option. I had no one to cover for me if I started feeling sick, and this ride was double the time. Thus, the dread.

Those nasty comparisons began to seep back into my head. While I was driving around feeling sick, what would the other moms be doing? Exercising? Meeting a friend for coffee? Ah yes, envy has a way of wiggling in. I didn't blame them for using their time in these ways, I just wanted to join them!

The party began with the 1st graders noticing rods at the top of the bus and using them like monkey bars. Soon enough the bus was filled with children hanging from the ceiling. Then the disco lights swirled and the music pounded the walls. Lukas smushed his ears with his hands as he desperately battled his sensory processing issues. Then he frantically burrowed his head into his backpack, scrambling to retrieve his iPad. *Oh, no, we didn't come on this bus for you to be glued to an iPad! We could do that at home.* And with the iPad quickly hidden away, we both had to face our dread of entering the chaos.

It was then that a classmate came to the rescue. He grabbed Lukas' hands, and they began dancing alongside the others. Lukas was jumping and laughing and that pure joy was once again in the air!

At the trampoline party, I had to start the jumping in

order to encourage Lukas to join in; at this party, he started the jumping and I soon joined in. I was again given a front row seat to my son's delight.

What began with me feeling like I was the only parent who had to come on the bus, transformed into me feeling like I was the only parent lucky enough to come on the bus. I no longer sat still trying to protect my wayward stomach, I was now up on my feet dancing with seven-year-olds to "Who Let the Dogs Out?"

God turns our mourning into dancing—I remember learning that from the Bible—and there I was witnessing how he could turn my moaning into dancing. I had been invited to bury dread in order to discover delight.

Chapter 37

The Mantra

"Fear or faith?"—this mantra God gave me when Lukas was soon to face heart surgery would continue to re-emerge. Although Lukas gave birth to many of my fears, he has also taught me how to live more fearlessly. The tension between these words remains; however, I want faith to hold the melody line so that fear becomes merely a hushed voice in the background.

Our move from Chicagoland to Florida, leaving both of our families, friends from childhood, and the hometown we both grew up in was possible because we were learning how to prevent fear from looming too large. And adopting Sarah in the midst of this stressful move may have felt unfathomable if it weren't for this mantra remaining fresh in my spirit.

I was well acquainted with how fear suggested I stay small or in my own corner. But a theater game I loved to play with my actors, called "Kitty Wants a Corner," beckoned me to defy fear in order to experience the beauty of risk-taking. The premise is everyone stands in a circle with one person designated to the center. This center player runs to someone in the circle and says, "Kitty wants a corner." A person lining the circle responds by saying, "Go see my neighbor." Then the center player chooses a new person in the circle and repeats his given phrase of "Kitty wants a corner," only to hear the same response every time: "Go see my neighbor."

The game is very boring at first glance. However, there is more. The main action is to switch places with someone in the circle. You make eye contact with a player across the way, when the center player isn't looking, and then you dart across the circle to her spot as she runs to yours. The goal is to make it to your partner's place before the center person steals it and leaves one of you as the new center player.

Typically, the game begins with very few people exchanging places. Everyone is extremely cautious and the game feels sluggish. After a while of this, I ask the cast what they think this game teaches. Usually I hear things like, "non-verbal communication," or "working off of each other." But then I ask them if the game is more fun on the sidelines, protecting your space, or tearing across the circle and potentially losing your space? They always know the answer. The adrenaline and joy are all found in the risk-taking, leaving the safety of known ground to rush across and claim new ground.

I tell them the reason I play this game on the first day of rehearsal is that our journey as actors is about taking risks. It is daring to move to places beyond ourselves that don't always feel safe or sure. Nevertheless, we need to notice how we become more courageous and willing to take risks the more we take them. Once we have experienced how risk-taking stretches us in profound ways, we start to yearn for more of these experiences.

I think life is a lot like this game. We can reason that moving into unfamiliar territory is not worth the risk, so we stay rooted to our initial place. We might even assure ourselves that we can still enjoy the game as we watch from the sidelines. But once we give ourselves the permission to fail, to run across the circle knowing we may lose our once familiar spot, we begin to learn that this is when we come alive. These are the actors that are yelping with laughter and dancing when they triumphantly arrive in a new place. It is in our practice of taking risks that we slowly bat down our tendencies to allow fear a stranglehold. I play this game as a touchstone for my actors, and I play this game as a touchstone for myself.

When those voices of fear emerge, Lukas' life reminds me to come back to "Fear or Faith?" And those same voices remind me of the profound lessons found in this simple theater game. Will I choose fear that tempts me to stay small? Fear that suggests I keep Lukas' feet in known territory rather than exploring the unknown. Fear that says I may not be able to navigate my way in a new space so I should stay rooted to the old. Or will I choose faith? Faith that invigorates me as we launch into new arenas. Faith that reminds me life can be much grander than I imagine on my own. Faith that awakens me and quickens me with joy.

I saw a similar principle in the study of literature when I taught the difference between dynamic and static characters. Dynamic characters were far more interesting to study because their life journeys were complex and vibrant; they were significantly transformed by the end of the story. For example, Sydney Carton from *A Tale of Two Cities* starts as a downcast, dissolute man, but after his own risk-taking, he becomes an engaged, self-sacrificing man. If these dynamic characters were the ones that captured my attention, why did I sometimes live like I wanted to be a static character, safe and unchanged? Like I wanted to be one of the actors who maintained her corner rather than someone who sought out new ones? Like my highest goal for Lukas was that he stayed safe rather than experienced the wide range of life?

I suppose we all want a corner. But we most often need to face our fear and take a risk in order to find those corners that are life-giving. Lukas beckons me to fight off those voices of fear, so we both can experience the exhilaration that comes along with daring. Failure may await...but I think we will be glad we risked anyway.

Chapter 38

Marriage: Shared, Divided, and Multiplied

Before Eric and I were married, a good friend of ours gave us two pieces of advice: "Make sure you keep dating. And, alternate who plans your anniversary celebrations—one of you takes the even years and the other takes the odd ones."

We were particularly excited to try this anniversary pattern. If all of the planning fell on Eric, I knew he might tire of it. I could almost envision how this story would write itself. Eric's joy around planning fun celebrations would eventually wane until he started to say, "Do you want to just order in and watch a movie?" Then I would step in and become the head planner, disappointed that I no longer felt wooed. Yes, alternating would be much better. It would give us the opportunity to be both the bearer and receiver of the gift.

This back and forth is the rhythm we have had to find in our parenting of Lukas. We have had to be very intentional about knowing when to take the lead and when to ask for rest. We are constantly having discussions around "What do you need? How can I help?" And "This isn't working for me; I need you to step into this place and provide some relief." Lukas is very fluid in his behaviors, always finding new ways to capture our attention, so we have to revisit these conversations often.

Since Lukas demands a lot of care, we could easily be swept up into pouring all of our attention on him. But as I heard long before I met Eric, the best gift we can give our children is a good marriage. This means we have to pull away from Lukas at times in order to heed that other piece of advice we were given..."date often." Although guilt might try to sneak in about leaving our children with a babysitter for a night or a weekend, I choose to listen to that other voice who sweetly whispers, "Go." Spend time away rediscovering Eric. Learn what currently speaks to his soul. Go fall in love with him again. Blare music and sing together. Laugh at his jokes that also make him laugh. Hold his hand, kiss him deeply, linger in bed. This time away is not only kindness to each other, but also to Lukas...it gives him an opportunity to be loved by more people.

There is a low-grade fatigue that can happen with raising Lukas. We all know we are never at our best when we are tired. Perhaps this is a contributing factor to the divorce rate that plagues so many families raising children with special needs. Most days it feels impossible to shoulder the task of raising Lukas alone; consequently, Eric and I are braided together more tightly because of our need for one another. I have learned that I can either choose to see this need as a weakness or as a way we create deeper grooves in our marriage.

Eric has seen sides of me I tried to hide even from myself. But because of Lukas, Eric has loved me in those unlovable places. When we were dating, it was all about being loved for our strengths. I just wanted to reveal those places that felt very lovable, that would draw Eric closer, and that others had already affirmed. But with Lukas, we are often faced with loving each other in our weaknesses, which feels closer to the way I experience Jesus' love. Jesus loves me when I feel unlovely and in those places that feel unlovely. He invites *all* of me to the relationship, not just the polished parts.

And that is what Lukas has done in our marriage. He has caused us to witness all of who we are with each other. It is much more comfortable only revealing those more acceptable parts of me; however, I have slowly learned to bless this magnifying glass because it has allowed me to be more fully loved by Eric and invited me to love Eric more fully as well.

So yes, Lukas has revealed some of those shadowy parts of ourselves to each other. But he has shined a light on beautiful parts as well. I have witnessed Eric's powerful gentleness. He is quick to wrap his arms around Lukas when Lukas is spiraling into negative behavior. Eric resets him with love. And I have witnessed Eric's ability to bump up against difficult places in life and be strangely energized by each new challenge. Perhaps it springs from his baseball years. Rather than shrinking from difficult odds, he views them as a great opportunity to rally anew. I see this side of him emerge when we encounter those tricky moments with Lukas.

I also continue to learn from Eric's "come as you are" nature. Eric doesn't get embarrassed by Lukas' behavior or apologize for it, he simply says: "That's Lukas." He welcomes all of Lukas. I love watching this because I know how much it means to me as he offers me the same widespread arms. In some ways, it brings me back to those words at our wedding. "I choose you." We didn't just choose parts of each other to love. It was as if we were saying: "I choose ALL of you."

When I think about how our marriage has been impacted by raising Lukas, it has to do with how we see each other. After a recent visit to the eye doctor, I learned that they were giving me two different strengths on my contacts. One eye would help me with distance and one eye would help me with reading. That is how Eric and I parent together. We need to find places where we can build in distance and the chance to honor each other's need to rest and refuel. And we need to remember the gift we have of seeing each other up close, reading each other's souls with deeper vision.

It is rooted in that beautiful word "and." It is giving space *and* holding on to each other. It is establishing rhythms *and* rewriting those rhythms as often as needed. It is more peeks into those places where we feel unlovely *and* more marveling at those moments when we see each other's greater beauty revealed.

An adaptation of an old Swedish proverb says: "A suffering shared is a weight divided and a joy shared is a delight multiplied."

That sounds a lot like parenting Lukas.

That sounds a lot like being married to Eric.

Chapter 39

Only in Hindsight

If someone asked me to name my favorite movies, I would include *Of Mice and Men, What's Eating Gilbert Grape, Dominic and Eugene, Forest Gump, Rain Man,* and *I Am Sam*. I would have shared this list long before Lukas was born. This list of movies suggests I shouldn't be surprised that I have a child with DS and ASD. Each movie explores the world of someone with a mental deficiency or neurological disorder and the beautiful relationship that emerges when a person comes beside him. It just doesn't feel like coincidence that I loved these movies before having Lukas; it feels more like they were seeping into my soul as a preparation for what was to come.

We can only understand some aspects of our life in hindsight. As I looked back, I noticed a few other things that prepared the soil of my heart for Lukas. When I was doing my student teaching at New Trier High School in Winnetka, IL, I was asked to be an assistant coach for their speech team. One of the new members was a young man named Brad who had cerebral palsy. He was in a wheelchair and had limited speech, but he had a strong desire to learn a monologue and perform it. His blurred diction would make it difficult for judges to understand him, but his impassioned performance would surely give them a peek into his spirit. After working with around twenty students that year, Brad is the only name that remains with me. His humor, courage, and desire that was unconfined by his limitations were just some of the ways he crept into my heart.

About ten years later, when I was in my last years at this same high school, there was a young girl, Abby, who wanted to join an advisery group. An advisery was a group of twenty-five girls who met every morning and walked through high school together. This program was designed to make a school of 4,000 students feel more personable. Due to Abby's special needs, she hadn't been assigned an advisery. Like Brad, she also was confined to a wheelchair as she had no use of her arms or legs. With her chin, she would tap a button on her wheelchair to activate messages her aide had pre-recorded. Thus, conversations with her were very limited.

When we first welcomed Abby into our advisery, I noticed I was the only one who had daily interactions with her. Most days she would just sit and observe the girls around her, while they simply carried on as if she wasn't there. Abby faded into the background. Since the hope was for her to interact with girls her age, I was the one who needed to fade into the background. Thus, I decided to set up a "coffee date" schedule that paired two girls with Abby each morning. I needed to help the girls get over any hesitation or fear of interacting with Abby if these relationships were ever going to emerge. These coffee dates would be our way to *start with our toes*.

The girls probably felt like I was forcing their hand a bit with this tactic, but I also knew that sometimes "mandatory fun" leads to that same fun becoming self-initiated in the future. So each day Abby joined us, she had two girls who sat with her and tried to get to know her. Eventually we faded out the coffee schedule and girls went to Abby on their own. There were days when a girl would brush Abby's hair or grab toys to play with her. We all were learning how to better interact with Abby, and we soon realized how special she made our group. We were getting stretched beyond ourselves. Abby was making our day as we feebly tried to do the same for her.

I love looking back and witnessing how these movies paved the way for Lukas' arrival. How Brad and Abby paved the way. It was God shining a small light on what was to come. When we aren't exposed to people who are different from us, we never learn how to interact with them. And then fear builds those walls.

But God goes before us. He started writing a story on my heart long before Lukas, and it is one I have really only noticed in hindsight. It is a story of loving those who tend to be overlooked or forgotten. There is something gentle about His ways. I can now see that he didn't pop circumstances on me as much as He prepared pathways for me. He gardened the soil of my heart because He knew the seeds that would someday be planted.

Chapter 40

The Unnamed Ingredients

Motherhood. That word is painted with an amber glow. The image of a mother rocking her child by the fire springs to mind. Other images I associate with motherhood are captured on magnets that line the side of our refrigerator. I was given them as a gift when I became pregnant. Some of the scenes include a mother gently washing her child's feet in a basin, a daughter curled up with her mother as she plays the mandolin, and a mother with a child nestled into her neck. All of these images have an ease to them. However, in my experience, mothering hasn't been about ease.

Upon reflecting, I realized how fear stood at the beginning of both our children's lives. With Lukas, it was the fear of the unknown. What medical issues would he face? How would Down syndrome impact his development? Would he have to struggle for acceptance? With Sarah, it was the fear of whether or not we would be a good fit for each other. Were we the best family for her? Would she and Lukas genuinely get along? What shifts would occur when she learned we weren't her biological parents?

But to stop there only provides an incomplete picture

because once I acknowledged my fears, joy emerged. Joy as Lukas made strides in the most breathtaking ways. And joy as Sarah touched our lives beyond what we could have imagined. I guess my experience with motherhood is much more about "The And," a word that continues to help me process so much of life. Motherhood is beautiful *and* frightening. It is joyous *and* filled with pain. It far exceeds my expectations *and* it disappoints me. It fills me up *and* it depletes me. It makes me soar *and* it makes me stumble.

When I look at what mothering was like for Hannah from the Hebrew scriptures, I see that she, too, experienced both blessing and pain in motherhood. She begged God for a son, vowing to dedicate this child back to Him if only He would help her conceive. God answered her prayer through the gift of Samuel. However, after three short years, it was time to release this son back to God. From then on, she would only see Samuel once a year. This blessing was now tinged with loss. Hannah's bond with her child was one she had to learn to hold very loosely.

Another Biblical woman, Eve, received God's direction to multiply the earth. She must have been so curious—how could two people create another one? She didn't have the opportunity to glean from women who went before her. Instead, she was forging the way of motherhood and walking into completely unknown territory. I can only imagine the questions and fascination swirling around in her head. She was made in God's image, and since He is a creator, she, too, would have the opportunity to create.

Yet she also must have brimmed with fear as she faced this new journey. God told her she would experience great pain in childbirth. She entered this new role with wonder and dread standing side by side. After experiencing the miracle of creating life, Eve would soon be gripped by severe pain. One of her sons would kill the other one. This painting of motherhood, once only an image of intimacy, now had a gash of destruction on it. The colors of beauty had been marred by the colors of devastation.

Due to familiarity, the sting of that story may have lost its potency, but when we hear Mary Chapman (wife of musician Stephen Curtis Chapman) describe the harrowing day her son accidentally ran over their little daughter, we ache with pain. How could anyone endure the loss of a child by the hands of her other child? Eve experienced this unfathomable loss. Our first mother points us to this fuller view of motherhood: motherhood evokes great joy and it is cloaked in great pain.

And we can't look at mothering without also acknowledging Mary, the mother of Jesus. She is a mother who couldn't find her son for three days; I could hardly bear losing Lukas for thirty minutes. Yet that is a small loss compared to knowing her son came to die. A son tortured with stripes on his back that she couldn't care for, a son weighed down by a cross that she couldn't carry, and a son humiliated on that cross whom she couldn't console. She could only stand there as a witness to his suffering.

Mary's story reminds us that our presence is the gift we give our children in the midst of their pain. She couldn't save her son...that is what *He* came for. And we can't save our sons and daughters. But like Mary, standing beside her son when pain was excruciating and all the others trailed away, we have the opportunity to remind our children that they are not alone. We cannot save, but we can stand...right by their side.

Our role isn't to save our children from their pain. Their

pain and their wounds are what lead to their beauty—just like Jesus. He walked toward pain and suffering, so he could walk toward resurrection and glory. When Peter tried to spare Jesus the road of grief that lay ahead, Jesus proclaimed that Peter's fear needed to "stand back" so that a greater good could be revealed. We, too, need to ask the fears we encounter in motherhood to "stand back" so that our children can experience both joy and pain along the way.

Motherhood is a gift. This has been stated in countless ways. But what we haven't really acknowledged and named is that motherhood is a gift that has loss as one of its central ingredients. The loss of a baby face, the loss of unabashed affection, the loss of dependency, the loss of being the primary mentor, the loss of innocence, the loss of a life without pain.

Hannah experienced loss, Eve experienced loss, Mary experienced loss. And God experienced loss.

So why do it? Why subject ourselves to a role that will lead us into fear, pain, and so many kinds of loss? Because it also leads us to higher ground: We learn courage in facing our fears. We learn humility and community as we face our pain. We learn about resurrection as we experience loss.

And we learn love.

We have the honor of coming alongside our children and bearing witness to the emotions they will face. We witness how the simple can become sacred. How the most mundane of moments are holy because God has given us front row seats to watch lives that are transforming. It is the "Far, far better" I had imagined.

We can name the loss that is found in motherhood because gain sits at this story's end.

Chapter 41

Roll Call

I have always disliked the beginning of Matthew's gospel—the endless list of unfamiliar names: Jeconiah, Shealtiel, Zerubbabel, Abihud, to name a few. This was one of the first texts I was commissioned to teach in my AP Literature class, and I dreaded such a droll beginning. I knew it all held significance, but I likened it to reading attendance sheets on the first day of school. Lots of student names, but none with faces yet. My classroom roll call only became enjoyable once I knew my students' faces and more about them.

So it is with our own lives. If the various roles we take on remain generic or impersonal, then it is harder to feel engaged or fulfilled in these roles. However, once God ushers us into the process of naming who we are, then the ordinary becomes the unique. For example, my desire to answer the question: "What is a mother?" changed into the question: "Who am I as a mother?" A change from the general to the personal; a shift to living in my own lane.

There is something to this idea of naming. God changed people's names as a way of leading them to a higher calling on their lives: Abram became Abraham - Father of many nations, and Simon became Peter - the rock He would build His church upon. Jesus has many names since

His impact is so far-reaching (Good Shepherd, Bread of Life, Counselor, Deliverer, to name a few). The point is Jesus didn't come as a generic son. He came with a fingerprint and mission all His own, and his various names help reveal the specificity of who He is.

And out of all of God's servants that we meet in the Hebrew scriptures, only one of them named God. In the book *Inspired*, Rachel Held Evans writes:

> "Most of the time, God does the naming. Abraham. Isaac. Israel. Just one person in all your sacred Scripture dared to name God, and it wasn't a priest, prophet, warrior or king. It was I, Hagar—foreigner, woman, slave.... You are a God who not only hears, but also sees...I have seen the One who sees me. So I named God...El Roi, the God Who Sees."

Hagar's experience in the wilderness enabled her to know God better, and she named what all of us yearn to affirm: God isn't detached and unaware of our day to day lives. No, He is the God who sees. To know God in this way makes a profound difference. The name Hagar gave Him revealed a specific attribute that set Him apart from other gods. Naming gives all of us a specific mission.

As you know, we labored long before the labor of childbirth to name our son. His name speaks to so much of what this journey has been...a walk from darkness into light, from heaviness to lightness. In the novel *When the Heart Waits*, Sue Monk Kidd names what our experience has felt like. "Julian of Norwich wrote that our wounds become the womb. This touching image points us to the awareness that transformation hinges on our ability to turn our pain (the tomb) into a fertile place where life is birthed (the womb)." The tomb and darkness became the womb and light. The cloak that veiled our ability to see life in deeper ways was pierced by Lukas and a pinhole remains.

A name awaits us all. I think it goes beyond the name our parents gave us. I want to hear the name God whispers over me. I have witnessed this with people in my midst. It could be like Arloa Sutter who might be named "open door" as she welcomed those who needed a place for sustenance and sleep. Her open-door policy turned into a stunning Chicago outreach called Breakthrough Urban Ministries, which serves those affected by poverty. Or it could be "fisherman" like an elderly man at our church who walks around with goldfish in his pockets so he can connect with kids. He has captured Lukas' heart by showing great interest in one who could easily feel forgotten. These are not generic servants. They are people who have discovered God's name for them so their unique fingerprint can be placed upon this world. Our name is not on a long roll call where we bear no face; God knows our names and He sees us...now we get to accept the invitation to see ourselves like He does.

So what name has God been whispering over me through my children? I am still in that discovery process, but I will know it one day. John tells us in Revelations that God will give us a white stone with a new name written on it. For now, I continue to listen. God has breathed life into dark places and so much has been redeemed in me through my children. And those aching places that have not yet been redeemed are simply that—*not yet*. Like Lukas, I live in the ellipsis...what is yet to come. The grammatical marking of a period suggests a finality. It is done. Those words are reserved for Jesus. My life isn't marked by completion; it is marked by continuation. In fact, just as I think I have dealt with a wound or an issue, I soon learn there is another layer to unravel. The ellipsis reminds me that there is always more to come.

Although I started these writings as my way to honor and better know Lukas, God has shown me that they were also a way of better knowing myself. This little light of mine's brilliance has led me back home. I started by birthing him and he has joined the conversation by also birthing me.

Chapter 42

The Great Physician

Yes, Luke is my favorite gospel writer. He is the writer I have gravitated toward because he gives Jesus' fullest narrative, from birth to death. He also includes some of my favorite stories that don't appear in the other gospels: the story of Martha bustling about while Mary chooses "what is better" and sits at Jesus' feet, the thief on the cross who Jesus tells he will see again in Paradise, the story of the ten lepers and the one who returned with a grateful heart, and the touchstone story of grace found in the Prodigal son.

As a physician, I imagine that Luke was particularly drawn to Jesus' role as a healer. They shared a common desire to make others well. Since Lukas shares a name with this gospel writer, I have felt compelled to ask myself: How has Lukas made me well?

I started this journey feeling quite sick, wondering if Lukas was a punishment or a present? What were the ways that I had gone astray that may have led God to give me a consequence? The thought tears into my heart even now. I had to wrestle with the question of how Lukas could be a punishment, even as he bore God's image. Since God's image is about life, not death, Lukas was about life, not death. The idea of punishment quickly faded into the heap of lies we all have to sort through. Life is to be celebrated and this would inform how I walked forward.

Even though there was sadness when we first learned Lukas had Down syndrome, joy seeped into those broken cracks. The movie *Inside Out* beautifully illustrates the unique relationship between Sadness and Joy (two characters in the movie). The main character, Riley, missed the winning shot at her hockey playoff game, so she fell into deep sadness. Her parents and teammates "came to help because of sadness" and gathered around her. This scene ends with Riley being lifted high above their heads. Not because Riley could celebrate a winning shot, but because she could celebrate how her sadness and their love knit them together. Sadness preceded great joy. Instead of keeping Sadness confined inside a circle, as Joy tried to do, she had to let Sadness touch moments in Riley's life because sadness ushered in community. This has been our experience as well. Our family and friends helped us process the unexpected so we could eventually transform our grief into joy.

In a New Testament story, Jesus heard a blind man crying out for mercy as He passed by. Jesus called him to draw near and asked, "What do you want me to do for you?"

"Lord, I want to see," the blind man replied.

Jesus said to him, "Receive your sight, your faith has made you well."

I think Lukas has done that for me; he has given me new sight and sent me on a journey towards deeper wellness. He has torn my heart, widened it, and made me choose faith when it didn't even feel possible. I have undergone my own kind of heart surgery because of him. I have new scars because of our story together, but they beckon me back to the heart of Jesus. How did his disciples know who he was when he returned after the resurrection? They knew him by his scars. He held out his pierced hands and showed his cut side so they would know Him.

We, too, need to know each other by our scars; they are the marks that tell our story. And better yet, they are the marks that tell God's story. So rather than trying to cover them up as we are prone to do, God invites us to share them. To step out in faith. Like the healed blind man, I am learning that the faith required of me on this journey will slowly make me well.

We all have a Lukas in our midst—someone who is different from us, maybe scary to approach, someone who counters our society's whispers to surround ourselves with people who are accomplished, intellectual, and beautiful. Maybe what our soul needs is a break from that. Maybe we need to encounter someone who falls short on those accounts, but whose life is the profound reminder that he or she is worthy nonetheless; just as we are worthy without any external striving. We are worthy *just because*. We are the creation God named *very good* before any striving took place.

Lukas and all those others "out on the street" have great worth and are just waiting for us to go out and meet them. The great physician may not be in the immaculate, ordered office; instead, he may be out in the chaotic, lively streets. The whispers to "come outside" are worth listening to—you will find treasures in the most unexpected places.

I know. It is where I found Lukas.

Epilogue

So how did I come upon the title *Beside You*?

Our journey has been about recognizing the ways that Jesus has come to sit beside us. There is such tender love in this gesture. It can cause me to curl up or crumple beside Him. Or, it can embolden me with renewed strength. Whatever the response may be, my deepest hope has always been to experience His nearness.

This is also the story of how I have been invited to sit beside Lukas. In those difficult moments. In those moments of wonder and joy. In those moments that seem so mundane yet soon reveal their hint of glory.

And my hope has been to sit beside all of you who have walked a similar path. Together we get to bear witness to the wide range of moments life gives us.

So these were the musings that led to my title, but what about the subtitle? How has sitting beside Lukas revealed my own special needs? And what are those special needs I discovered along the way?

I learned I have the essential, dare I say, dire need to ask others for help. This asking runs so counter to the narrative we have inherited: America loves independence. Although we may want to do it single-handedly, we often need the same "hand over hand" help that someone like Lukas needs.

Living in community is another need I have. One need

grows upon the other and I am more willing to ask for assistance once I acknowledge that my call for help tends to build connections. It is about gathering a table of people who will walk with us on our journey. Just as Lukas has an OT, ST, BT, ESE teacher at his IEP meetings to help guide his educational journey, I, too, need a "table of people" with different gifts and perceptions to help light my way.

I also learned that my imperfections are not occasions for shame, but an opportunity to bless rather than berate how I may fall short. Growth awaits me when I embrace those parts of myself that I may be tempted to disown. As Leonard Cohen said, "There is a crack, a crack in everything / That's how the light gets in."

Lastly, I have the need to reorient to love, to the Divine. In the midst of desiring control and mastery, I can miss the beautiful child standing right before me. Somehow, I am surprised when the Spirit reminds me I am not the potter. God just invites me to put my hands on the clay with Him as He guides the molding: smoothing this part out, adding more substance here, removing what is no longer needed. And when I whisper that I am weary or feeling too small for the task, I am ushered back to the Sacred who multiplies the fish and bread. Our mere crumbs become a feast in His hands. Our special needs lead us to that breathtaking table.

Thank You

Let me start where this journey all began...standing beside Eric.

To Eric—You not only see my heart when I share it, but also when it is in hiding and needs to be seen all the more. You keep me from sinking on those deeply discouraging days, and you join me in delight when Lukas takes those small, BIG steps. I love holding your hand on both of these occasions. I choose you again & again.

To Mama and Dad—your love of standing by each other's side for 55 years is breathtaking. You gathered me and my brothers around that deep well and taught us how to love one another. We took our "last family trip" multiple times because we just kept wanting to be together. Mama, you savor the moment; Dad, you see and create beauty...how I long to do both in my mothering of Lukas and Sarah. Thank you for loving me in the muck, but never leaving me there. Your outstretched hands were always etched with hope.

To Brett and Jason—my childhood is filled with memories of creating together, finding ways to bring our insides to the outside. You buoy me with your humor and tenderness. Life is infinitely better with you by my side.

To my early readers, even amidst the messiness, you helped me uncover a way and guided me to better paths: Tiffin Bolger, Jean Masukevich, MaryBeth Jackson, Dan LaMorte, Juliet Blumenthal, Rob Boncosky, and Haley

Harris—your friendships are so inviting and true that you felt like safe places to leave this story and my heart. Thank you for being beautiful harbors.

To E.M. Forster who said: "How do I know what I think until I see what I say?" His words nudged me to uncover what I was thinking and begin the writing process.

To Jessica Parker, Ina Baker, and the team at BookLogix. You made the final stretch of this process such an inviting collaboration.

To all those who have loved Lukas with a tender fierceness. Thank you for both pouring into him and drawing out of him—you each reveal sides of Lukas that make him more vibrant and full.

Steven, Holly, Kurtis, and Sarah.
Grammy and Papa.
Nana and Papa Joe.
Aunts, Uncles, and Cousins.
Teachers and Therapists.

You are all light in his life.

To Lukas, this is my love letter to you. You bring me to the deep. It has been a beautiful epiphany to discover that I needed your hand to take me there.

And to the Sacred, You are a wind that breathes life into those hidden places. You inspire, inform, and illuminate my steps…the nearness of God has always been my good.

An Afterword

Since this memoir was written over a period of years, things have changed along the way. I thought it was important to capture just a few of those changes for you...

I have learned that people-first language is important in some circles and hurtful in others. In the Down syndrome community, we use a "Nouns First" mentality. However, in the deaf community (to select just one example), they prefer to be addressed as "a deaf person" rather than "a person who is deaf." Since being deaf is such an essential part of who they are, they want the language to reflect that. It is important for us to learn the heartbeat of each disabled community; their desires don't fit neatly into one universal mold (The Lucky Few podcast episode 88 addresses this).

During the Covid 19 season, Lukas moved to a different learning model. He went to his home school for a portion of the morning, but then spent the majority of his day learning at his ABA therapy clinic. We saw how he thrived in this atmosphere, even though he wasn't receiving the same level of inclusion that is important to us. It has reminded us to stay fluid in this educational process. We continue to hold specific goals for Lukas' life, but he joins the conversation, and we want to learn where he is thriving. Each season may hold something different, so we continue to keep our palms open rather than clenched around a preconceived notion of how this all should unfold.

Toilet training continued to take its toll on us. After trying all kinds of charting and a variety of motivators, what finally worked seemed so unexpected. His behavior therapists had recently purchased the "Yes, No, Sorry, Maybe" Sound Buttons and Lukas became enamored with them. So we tried implementing these as his toileting reward and to all of our surprise, they worked. Was it finally finding the right thing or finally finding the right timing? After trying to mastermind it all, we are simply left saying we don't know. However, in celebration, my brother sent us another button. When you push it, it says: "That was easy." The discrepancy is not lost on us, but we can finally laugh and celebrate anyway!

Mitch from "Walls Won't Win" has become one of the dearest boys to Lukas. The young boy on that soccer field is now one who embraces and even champions Lukas. Kindness won.

Here is what has been true all along: People with Down syndrome are worth learning from, fighting for, standing with, and believing in. They exude a humanity that can make us all more in touch with our own humanity.

Endnotes

CHAPTER 2: GREAT EXPECTATIONS
1. Charles Dickens, *A Tale of Two Cities* (London: Penguin Classics, 2000), 390.

CHAPTER 4: NOUNS FIRST
1. Kathryn Lynard, ed, *Gifts: Mothers Reflect on How Children with Down Syndrome Enrich Their Lives* (Bethesda: Woodbine House, Inc, 2006).

CHAPTER 5: MANNA FOR THE DAY
1. Moses and manna -- Exodus 16:4-5; Exodus 16: 15-16
2. "You will keep in perfect peace…" -- Isaiah 26:3 (NIV)

CHAPTER 7: THE LURKING MONSTER
1. Ann Voskamp, The Broken Way: A Daring Path to the Abundant Life (Grand Rapids: Zondervan, 2016), 91.

CHAPTER 9: FOR NOTHING IS IMPOSSIBLE WITH GOD
1. "For nothing is impossible with God" -- Luke 1:37 (NLT)

CHAPTER 12: PULL UP A CHAIR
1. Parable of the Great Banquet -- Luke 14:16-24

CHAPTER 14: SILENTLY SPEAKING
1. Zechariah's story -- Luke 1:5-22 and 57-64

CHAPTER 15: SPECIAL NEEDS INDEED
1. Ann Voskamp, The Broken Way: A Daring Path to the Abundant Life (Grand Rapids: Zondervan, 2016), 25.

CHAPTER 16: RE-MEMBER
1. Daniel Keyes, *Flowers for Algernon*, (Boston: Mariner Books, 1994), 161.
2. "Studies Demonstrate Link among Alzheimer's Disease, Down Syndrome and Atherosclerosis." n.d. ScienceDaily. Accessed October, 2019. https://www.sciencedaily.com/releases/2010/01/10 0115182639.htm.
3. "People with Down Syndrome are Pioneers in Alzheimer's Research." n.d. NPR.org. Accessed September, 2019. https://www.npr.org/sections/healthshots/2014/08 /25/341672950/people-with-down-synd.

CHAPTER 19: MIRRORED PAIN
1. Albert Camus, *The Stranger* (New York: Vintage International, 1989).

CHAPTER 22: ABANDON
1. "He will not leave you or abandon you" -- Deuteronomy 31:6 (CST)
2. Jesus with disciples in Gethsemane -- Matthew 26:36-46

CHAPTER 23: ARMOR OF GOD
1. Armor of God -- Ephesians 6: 10-18
2. Leanna Tankserley, *Begin Again: The Brave Practice of Releasing Hurt and Receiving Rest* (Grand Rapids: Revell, 2018), 135-6.

CHAPTER 27: KIND TO OUR CORE
1. Tennessee Williams, *A Streetcar Named Desire* (Sewanee, TN: The University of the South, 1957), 178.
2. "Love your neighbor as yourself" – Matthew 22:36-39 (NIV)
3. "A Little Bit of Love" by Paul Williams

CHAPTER 28: WEIGHTY MATTERS
1. "It was very good" -- Genesis 1:26-31 (NIV)

CHAPTER 29: TRAINING FOR TWO CONTINUES
1. The Battle of Jericho -- Joshua 6:2-16

CHAPTER 30: STABLE SITTING
1. Frederich Buechner, *Now & Then: A Memoir of Vocation*, 1st ed. (New York: Harper & Row, 1983), 55-56.
2. Valley of Dry Bones -- Ezekiel 37:1-14

CHAPTER 32: LIVING IN YOUR LANE
1. Parker Palmer, *Let Your Life Speak: Listening for the Voice of Vocation* (San Francisco: Jossey-Bass, 2000), 55.
2. Many body parts, one body -- I Corinthians 12:12-26 (NLT)

CHAPTER 34: BEAUTY IN THE WADING
1. The Prodigal son -- Luke 15:11-32

CHAPTER 35: CALL OF THE ONE
1. Philip and the Ethiopian -- Acts 8:27-39

CHAPTER 38: MARRIAGE: SHARED, DIVIDED, AND MULTIPLIED
1. Swedish proverb: "A shared joy is a double joy; a shared sorrow is half a sorrow."

CHAPTER 40: THE UNNAMED INGREDIENTS
1. Mary Beth Chapman and Ellen Vaughn, *Choosing to SEE: A Journey of Struggle and Hope* (Grand Rapids: Revell, 2010).

CHAPTER 41: ROLL CALL
1. Rachel Held Evans, *Inspired* (Nashville: Nelson Books, 2018), 50, 53.
2. Sue Monk Kidd, *When the Heart Waits: Spiritual Direction for Life's Sacred Questions* (San Francisco: Harper, 2006), 155.

CHAPTER 42: THE GREAT PHYSICIAN
1. A blind man receives sight -- Luke 18:35-43
2. Jesus shows His pierced hands -- John 20:19-20
3. 2015. *Inside Out*. Film. Directed by Pete Docter. Pixar.

EPILOGUE
1. The potter and the clay -- Isaiah 64:8
2. The miracle of the five loaves and two fish – Matthew 14:15-21

"The light shines in the darkness, and the darkness has not overcome it" (John 1:5).

Glossary

DS............... Down syndrome

ASD............. Autism spectrum disorder

AV canal....... Atrioventricular canal

ABA............. Applied Behavior Analysis

EI................. Early intervention

OT............... Occupational therapist/therapy

ST................ Speech therapist/therapy

BT................ Behavior therapist/therapy

ESE.............. Exceptional student education

IEP.............. Individualized education program

DCFS........... Department of children and family services

About the Author

Kimberly Sanders attended Indiana University and received her BA in English & Theater. Later she received her Master of Arts in Teaching from Wheaton College. She worked as an actress in Chicago and then taught high school English for fourteen years. She integrated those passions when she adapted & directed literary works for the stage. She now leads Listen to my Life groups in Sanibel, FL, where she currently lives with her family.

She loves homemade gifts, a great round of Taboo, unsettling documentaries, backroads and 70's music with Eric, and dance parties with her children!